POEMS ON EVERY PAGE

MEIYIN GEORGIADES

DEDICATED TO:

MY FAMILY

Thank you so much for leading me towards God daily. Thank you for supporting me even when I didn't want it. Thank you for being the ones I can always turn to.

About the Author:

Meiyin is a Christian- a Christ follower- and attends 360 church. She is fluent in sarcasm and loves to bring smiles and laughs to people's day. Meiyin's hobbies are drawing, writing, and doing whatever activity peaks her interest at the moment. She loves traveling to different places, hiking, and photography. Meiyin enjoys working in the yard as her dogs play chase and wrestle.

FAITH

DAILY REPLAY #1

You say that I'm special just the way that I am.
But I don't really feel it,
I want to but can't.

The people around me run circles 'round my head.
I want to keep up,
But they're too fast,
I said.

I want to play music,
Compose,
And arrange.
But these are gifts you've not given me,
and I know I can't change.

I want to draw and paint photos for you.
But I can't do that either.

Why can't I?

Can you?

You can easily do all these things that I said.
You can give me these gifts,
But you say no instead.
I want to be special,
But I don't feel that way.

So why God?
So why,
Am I plain as a page?

I can do things that others can't.
Yes,
That is true.

I read the sheet music and play by it too.
But that is not talent,
It's learned instead.
And that is not special,
It's inside that's read.

I can't play a tune I hear off the bat.
I can't solve hard equations no matter the facts.
I can't draw a good picture by imagination alone.
I can't find a speck amiss in the tone.

I want to be special.
I want to be unique.
But for some reason,
I cannot find what it is that I seek.

Daily Replay #2

They say for us to keep busy.
But for me,
That is such a tizzy.
I'm here and then there,
But why should I care?
I'm busy with things that I like:

School and then practice and then practice some more homework is
such a chore.
Study for tests during my lunch...
Math numbers later to crunch.

Everything I do,
I do in a rush.
When will it become too much?

During my schedule,
I must find time,
And somewhere,
I must draw the line.

Some time without worry or without wait,
That is the day I await.

God says to help others that are in need,

And with that,
I fully agreed.

'Cause the lost appear like termites to wood,
And helping in ways that I could.

Someday it'll slow,
And I'll be alone.
That is the time that I dread.

But alone ain't a thing when I'm within His reach,
So I'll make the most of my life.

Daily Replay #3

I began my run with a negative mindset.

Ashes from my hopes lingered still.

The twists and turns made some lose hope,
but weren't too cruel to me.

I ran while my legs burned.
My breaths came out in turns.

As I ran up another hill,
My footfalls made a sound.

The ending was in sight.

A stretch so far,
It seemed.

My coach's voice yelled out to me,
Catch up with her ahead.

My mind was already in chains,
And I wanted to break free,
But my heart and my will held it still.

As the hurting within me spread its wings.
My breath comes out in bursts.
My legs felt no more.
My throat burned against the rush.

But I passed the red along the way.

The clock built up another second.
But I kept on going.
I did not stop.
So I had no regrets.

The raised black line met my mark.
And the world came back to me.

I was dizzy.
So I pulled off to the side.
The world blurred and spun.
But I had finished the race.

A long stretch and a strong finish and we hung out with unknown friends.

Ashes held against my heart warmed as the sun moved on.

Nobody is perfect.

Yet ash is perfect in imperfection.
If ash can overcome life itself.

What am I to be?

A.C.T.S Prayer

God loves me way more than I can see.

He loves me when I'm lost and when my boat is tossed.
He loves me when I'm hurt and when my sadness lurks.
He loves me when I'm blind and sees me when I'm fine.

Jesus is the:

Redeemer.
Blesser.
Shepherd.

He is the gate that I go through.
He is the vine that gives me life.
He is the light that guides me through.
He is gentle when I am harsh.

Jesus is perfect in every way.

My God is the true god.
Forever in His ways.

I have taken on too much.
And my hungry envy feeds.
I find it hard to stop and see all that I can do.

I don't set time aside to read the Word.

I don't get up to still the rushing flood.

I pray again that You'll help me be that way.

I thank You for this day and for the food on my plate.
Thank You for the people around me that you put here.
Thank you for the sky-blue days and the clouds passing through.

You gave me another day to glorify you.
So,
I will do my best.

I am way too ready to come home.
Help me to live in the moments.

Time to take for family makes my family wish that we didn't have so
much to do.
But that cannot come true.
We all like what we do and learn from activities.
But it isn't always good to be busy.

My friends at school see the grades that weigh so much.
The grades and sports and college begin to pile up.

Let them have a day to rest and not rush.

Let the world begin to see the glory of your works:

The blowing breeze.
The rustling trees,

And nature and its sound.

Let time slow.

Let them see.

Let it be for You.

FOLLOW

I will follow God.

Even in my uncertainty.
I will strive to find and understand Him.
Otherwise.
I need not live.

I will fall.
I will sink.

I will battle depression.
I will fight for my life.
I will search for my purpose.

I will not give up.
I will not swallow the pills.

I will reach out.
I will do my best.
I will confide in my friends.
I will learn what love is.
I will learn to understand the word "*family*".

I cannot give up.

I might have to fight harder for my life.

But I will.

I will.

GOD IS HERE

I'm weighted down right now by people's opinions.
Checking off their checklist for my life.
It's really strange to me why I'm doing this at all...
But maybe this is the best for my life.
I enjoy what I'm doing.
Making them my new hobbies.
But just around the bend,
The world waits for me.
All the challenges of this life...
But I know that God is here.

God is here.
I see Him in the breeze and the water and the trees.
He's in the birds and the grass and the rustling of the leaves.
I see Him right beside me guiding me through all of this.
Oh yes.
God's here.

I'm weighted down right now by the worries and the stress...
All the things I've got to get done.
The good grades and the prayer times.
It's just so much to do.
I want to play this perfectly for you.
Sometimes life feels like a twister pulling me away.
But of course.
I know that this isn't true.
But all the things in life can't be done to the letter.
I just can't do this alone.

All the worries and all the stress must leave me right now.
I want to get through all of this in one piece somehow.
The struggles in this life will melt away someday.
But until that day comes here is what I'll say.

God is here.
I see Him in the breeze and the water and the trees.
He's in the birds and the grass and the rustling of the leaves.
I see Him right beside me guiding me through all of this.
Oh yes.
God's here.

God has a plan and it might seem strange at first.
but who says we're supposed to know it all?
We are only human.
He is the Almighty.
Guess who has supreme control.
But God is not a genie who is here to grant my wishes.
but he wants the best for me.
When I am backed against the wall God is right beside me.
All I need to do is call for Him.

God is here.
I see Him in the breeze and the water and the trees.
He's in the birds and the grass and the rustling of the leaves.
I see Him right beside me guiding me through all of this.
Oh yes.
God's here.

God's Creations

The leaves shine green.
And the sky glows blue.
The clouds drift among the sky.
The sun glows bright.
And the moon gleams warmly.
God's creation sings:

Holy.
Holy is our Creator.
Greatest is He now.
All the wonders all around belong to Him.
Our God.

Flowers sprout among the grass.
The blue jay sings her songs.
The bees fly 'round.
And the wasps hum loudly.
The weeds grow beautifully.
The ponds are full of fish and birds.
Greatest are His works.

Holy.
Holy is our Creator.
Greatest is He now.
All the wonders all around belong to Him.
Our God.

The colorful clouds in the sky bring shade to us.
The people sing about God's grace.
Blessings in disguise.
Turtles move along the grass.
Rabbits hop in the brush.
Finding their young to love.
The tall grass blows.
And the trees grow tall.
Our God is talented.

Holy.
Holy is our Creator.
Greatest is He now.
All the wonders all around belong to Him.
Our God.

The breeze blows slow,
And our hearts beat fast.
God's creations are everywhere.
The air we breathe and the sky-blue days.
We take them for granted.
The new life brings lasting joy to all the people here.

The flower's scent and the bee's honey smell so sweet to us.
People declare God's name aloud.
How great is our life?
The people sing songs.
Pray.
And read God's will continuously.
Shadows dance along the walls.

Dancing to our life.

Holy.
Holy is our Creator.
Greatest is He now.
All the wonders all around belong to Him.
Our God.

Star's View

The stars look down upon this place,
Seeing all of this disgrace.
God put us here to live in peace,
But sin came in and changed some things.

God sent his one and only son to live among the peaceful ones.
Some tried to rid the world of Him.
But he stayed around and gained some friends.
Together they spread the word of God:
His joy and love and peace and such.
But they also warned of His justice:
Unbelievers sent away.

The stars see the troubled earth,
Once perfect without a flaw.
Alas,
Sin now taints this earth,
Yet beauty still remains.

God makes everything perfect in his eyes.
He sees all our pain and wishes it were gone.
Now's the time to turn to Him,
Away from all our sins.
To turn to His arms of grace and love,
And then our pain fades away.

Someday when His son returns,

The stars will shine with joy.
For the time of celebration.
For His followers is then.

But those who cast Him away.
And those who just don't care.
Will be cast away from His embrace to a very dark place.

But those who love and follow Him will go with the Lord to the place
where abundance flows.

And be forever with the Lord.

LIFE

Feelings locked away so tight.
Locked away from sight.

Lost.
I lost my way again.
I lost another friend.

Doubt.
Doubt is here again.
Doubt my old friend.

Oh.
When?
When will this make sense?

Lost without end.

Love that never fails is lost to me.

Oh.
Life.
Life is full of strife.
Life is full of sorrow.
So.
Wait and hold on until tomorrow.

A new day comes.

And the sun is shining bright.
The moon gleams silver tonight.
The stars blink slowly,
And my heart's so fast.

Now is the time to go.

Steps.
Daunting steps ahead.
And the darkness closes in.
Life is left behind,
And the darkness closes everything in sight.

Storm.
Wash away my fears.
Wash away my sorrows.
It is so so clear that there's hope for tomorrow.

The past is way back when.
So.
No need to look back for them.

It's time to move on,
And it's time to let them go.

Sun.
Look upon my face.
Take all my tears away.

'Cause now...

I want to start anew.
I want another try.
I want to have a good life without them by my side.

Oh God,
Pick me up.
Please.

Smile down upon me.
Bless me with your peace.
And bless me with this life.
I'm done with struggling against your will.

Oh God,
Your love for me runs deep.
Deeper than a canyon.
You care for me so much that it hurts in the slightest.
Stay by my side when hard things come my way.
Be my sword and shield when I have need for them.

Oh God,
Love me as you do:
Forever and ever.
And I will stick with you until the end.

Oh,
God...

<u>Here For You (God's P.O.V.)</u>

When hard things come your way,
Things turn dark and gray.

Your love for me begins to fail,
'Till in the depths too deep.

You sit alone,
Fearful of everything.

Lookin' left and lookin' right,
But when no one is in sight,
You turn away.

I'm here for you.
I'm waiting in the mist,
And the clouds,
And the sky.
In the morning and the night.
When you try to hide from me,
I see where you are.

You turned away from me,
Pleasing your friends,
But in the end,
It's the same.

Friends who aren't there when needed the most,

Just might be the wrong choice.

Lookin' around,
And no one is in sight.

The sky is dark as the night.

Your sight is clouded by the bad,
But I'm still here for you.

When you feel all alone in the dark,
When you feel like a speck of dust,

When you feel like you're lost,
In the twisting turns of life,
I will be your light.
I will find you.
I will guide you to my arms.

I'm here for you.
I'm waiting in the mist,
And the clouds,
And the sky.
In the morning and the night.
When you try to hide from me,
I see where you are.

Love

Hurt.
I'm backed against the wall.

Pain.
I can't see through the sorrow.

Love.
Tears me to shreds.

Oh.
When is tomorrow?

We love you.
We care.
Stay with us when the darkness comes around.

Love can hold the hurt.
But love can heal the sorrows.
Just hold on to your life until tomorrow.

Hold on to your life.
It's worth every second.

People who care are there for you.
So hold on to them tight.

Love can make you do the crazy.

Love can leave me so lonely,
But now's not the time to be sad.

God,
You hear my suffering and anguish.
You feel my pain and my loss.
You hear every prayer I send to you.

I know I should listen to you.
I know I should read your Word,
But you should know that I'm stumbling.

God,
What should I do?

They say to be true to yourself.
They say to show who you are,
But that is near to impossible because of who I am.

The chaos around me is deafening,
And it blocks off all my hope.
I know it's wrong,
But what should I do?

God,
I need your help.

You sent your son to earth to suffer and to save,
But did he get a label that he could not shake?

He loves me.
He cares.
He's here when darkness is around.
His love heals my hurt.
His love makes me welcome.

My God.

My Savior,

Jesus.

The Almighty

They say faith can move the highest mountain.
They say faith will lead you out of fear.
They say faith can do the impossible.
My God is always enough.

They say love can heal the broken.
They say love can heal the hurt.
They say love from God is forever.
My God is always enough.

But when my back is against the wall.
And the pain is brought upon me.
When I am broken on the floor.
His hand reaches out.

My God is the Almighty one.

Yes.
That is true.

He holds on to me tightly and doesn't let me go.
When I'm underneath the waves.
And drowning in the deep.
He reaches out to hold me and never lets me go.

When memories arrive,
And my heart breaks in two.
He is holding me tight to his chest.

When my friends walk away,
And when I'm all alone.
My life is burnt to ash as dark as night.

But as a phoenix rises.
I get a second chance to be reborn
and shine in His name.

My God is the Almighty one.

Yes.
That is true.

He holds on to me tightly and doesn't let me go.
When I'm underneath the waves.
And drowning in the deep.
He reaches out to hold me and never lets me go.

When challenges arise that some people just don't get.
I'm standing up for my God.

He sees me with my belief when stones are thrown.
Physical or not.
The stones hurt the same.

When darkness covers me,
And I can't see anything.
You help me to stand like a rock in my faith.
The Spirit burns in me,
And it's lighting up the darkness.
Everything it touches glows a bright light.

My God is the Almighty one.

Yes.
That is true.

He holds on to me tightly and doesn't let me go.
When I'm underneath the waves.
And drowning in the deep.
He reaches out to hold me and never lets me go.

The Perfect Place

Everything is laid in gold,
And smiles everywhere you go.
And everything is perfect.
Don't you see?

Kids run around the grass while parents smile and laugh.
Everything is perfect there,
You'll see.

Everything is changed a bit,
But don't you dare throw a fit.
Everything's the way it's meant to be.

One day when we grow old,
When colors all begin to grow,
That's when the world will fade away.
Then we will gain reward because of the life of our Lord Jesus.
He was laid down in sacrifice for us.
He died for us out of love.

And then we can enter the golden gates and gain some friends.
This is when everything will be just right.

No more pain or suffering.
No more fights or tears again.
Only the love of Jesus Christ.

We will get to know Him more.
And his father too.
The same.
Our LORD.
We will never go a second without them.

Happiness will not grow old,
And smiles will forever grow.

Everything is perfect there,
You'll see.

Set Free

When chains surround me,
And the light fades away.

When the storm within me takes all of my thoughts.

When the rain falls hard,
And the lightning strikes.

When tears mix with rain,
And the heart stops.

I'm here in the dark.

Alone with my thoughts.

Surrounded by sin.

The darkness takes all within.

But I've been *set free.*
I'm not alone.

God waits for me when I hide away.
He stands by my side,
And calls me home.
My home.

I've been set free.
I've been set free.

My Walk

Good morning God.
I've had my rest.
I know today I'll do my best.
Yesterday I knew I missed my mark.
Be with me when I'm in the dark.

You see all my hopes and fears.
You see all my dreams and tears.
You see every time I'm going down that road.
You see all my plastered smiles.
You hear all my fake worth-whiles.

Yet you stay by my side.
And you see me through.

Your love for me is great.
It's raining from the skies.
You shine through people near me.
And you act as my guide.

When I'm underneath the waves.
And when I'm drowning in the deep.
You throw a lifeline to me to grab before I sink.
As I go along this path of twisting and turning of heights and falls.
I need you beside me.
Or else I will fall.

Can't Stop

Another day passes without a fear in my mind.
Friends came on over,
And they lifted me up so high.
I spent today prepping for everything for tonight.
Everything went perfectly in my eyes.

The darkness below me wants to swallow me whole.
So,
When does this cycle of feelings ever slow?
Sometimes I'm high as the sun,
But sometimes,
I'm low as the ground that we stand on.

Where should I stand today?
Where should I stand right now?

Oh God,
I hear that you want all of me,
You want every single piece.
But that kinda terrifies me.
Will I lose who I am if I say yes to Your plan?

I can't stop.
I can't stop.
I can't stop,
Waiting for that feeling.

I can't stop.
I can't stop.
I can't stop.
Waiting for that star.

I can't stop.
I can't stop.
I can't stop.
Wanting to know more.
Wanting to get closer.
Get to know you.
LORD.

But I've been set free.
I'm not alone.
God waits for me when I hide away.
He stands by my side and calls me home.
My home.
'Cause now.
Now, I've been set free.

Black Skies

Black skies.
Black skies cover all the planes.
Black skies.
Black skies sing praises to your name.

The stars shine bright as a new day comes on high.
The angels sing God's name tonight.

Let's go.
Let go sing it on the mount'.
Spread the King's name around.
The time is now to go out into the world.
The little babe,
Jesus is born.

Second chances come with bright red bows.
Sing His praises while breath is in your lungs.

Bright stars.
Bright stars glitter in the sky.
Bright stars.
Bright stars sing Your name on high.

Heard. Seen. Done.

You hear my broken song.
You hear my weathered cry.
You hear my voice within the night.

You see my drying tears.
You see my sun go down.
You see my soul in tiny shreds.

Oh God.
You hear all that is for you.
And you hear all that is not.
You listen to my broken songs.
And my half-baked prayers.
And my wishes all in one.

You reach your hand out towards me.
You grab me by my wrist.
You pull me into your tight embrace.

The sun shines bright as I get another chance.
A chance to praise my LORD.
I feel the hope rising.
Arising in my soul.
Nothin' can hold me back no more.

No more.
No more.

The darkness cannot control me.
The weights can't hold me down.
The thoughts don't control my tongue.
No lustful ways will blind me.
No dreams will stop my roll.

WALKING

Walkin' down the highway.
Walkin' down the shore.
Finding the place to see You from the small earth below.

You see me.
You see me from your holy throne.
You see me down below.
I can find you as long as I do it right.
I can find you.
You're the light of my life.
The Light of my life.

I can walk along the shore.
I can walk past the water.
I leave behind a glow.
But yours is much brighter.
I can find the joy you bring,
It's louder than the sirens.
I can find the love you weave,
It's stronger than the fires.

I won't back down.
I'm stronger now.
With God.
I won't turn 'round.
He's leading me down the right path.

The Time is Now

There comes a time when you must choose and take your side.
There comes a time when you must stand up and fight.
There comes a time when you must find your voice.
When all you can do is say.
No more.

I've stood on my own two feet for so long.
I've stood on my own.
Fighting my way along.
I couldn't find the right path.
I couldn't find His voice.
But then you came along.
And I made my choice.

I stood up and I said.
No more.
I stood up and I said.
Walk out through that door.
I've made my choice.
And I'm saying.
Go away.
But still.
The voices taunt me night and day.

But you had come along and held my hand.
Suddenly.
I wasn't alone to stand.

I had a friend to help me through.
And now the devil can't ensnare me.

I stood up and I said.
Walk away.
I said.
Walk away and never come again.
I said.
Take the steps right out of my door.
And if you return I am not alone.

I'm not alone.
And I never have been.
God gave me people to help me through.
And now I've found the path that He wanted me on.
I'm not going to leave this path.
Never again.

The darkness may taunt me.
But I will take my stand.
I'll take it over and over again.
I'll do it for you, God.
I'll do it for you.

My friends stand up with me again and again.
There are no words that can say how grateful I am.
All I can say is.
Thank you.
Thank you.

Still.
The darkness may taunt me,
And frighten me too,
But I will take my stand.
I'll take it over and over again.
I'll do it for you, God.
I'll do it for you.

I found my voice.
I made my choice.
I'm not alone.

Contagious Light (God's P.O.V.)

You shine my light bright in the night.
Leading others to the light.
All shine with glorious light that chases away the darkness.
The walls crumble around you,
And all in a flash,
The darkness is gone.

The light keeps the darkness at bay.
But it finds a way to creep in when our light flickers.
You try to fight it on your own.
But it's too strong.
You start to sink beneath the waves.
And the happiness begins to fade.
But a hand reaches out.
You're pulled from the dark into the light.
You're embraced in loving arms.

All in a flash,
The darkness is gone.
Your walls crumble down.
You're now in the light.
Hope is shining so brightly.
The darkness stays away.
The darkness has been kept at bay.

GRAB ONTO HIS HAND

I was comfortable in this rut I called home.
I blended in with the darkness.
And there I roamed.
A canvas full of pain was written on my skin.
I longed for a day when the sun would come again.

A hand reached down towards me.
And there it stayed.
An aura of great light poured into my cave.

It took me a while to take His hand.
But when I grabbed on,
I felt alive again.

When the sun shone down upon my face,
My voice called out,
"Here,
Love abounds with grace."

Though it's better here to stand;
Struggles come and go again and again.

But wait,
There's a difference in what I face now.
For I am not alone.
We stand hand in hand.

Stand By You (God's P.O.V.)

I will stand by you.
I promise I'll see you through.
I'll light the way and prepare the day when you find yourself made new.

Here,
I stay.
You're loved always.
Come back to me,
And let me set you free.
I'll hold you tight when tears come 'night.
Let me light your world and cover your soul.

It only takes a seed to grow a tree,
And when you find me,
You'll finally be set free.
I'll guide you o'er hills full of grass and shield you from the darkness however long it lasts.
I'll be waiting when you turn away.
My arms are open wide with forgiveness and grace.

Here,
I stay.
You're loved always.
Come back to me,
And let me set you free.
I'll hold you tight when tears come 'night.
Let me light your world and cover your soul.

A Warning

Do you not hear the bays behind you?
Do you not hear the cackle of the devil?
Are you so brazen that you've become blind to where your path is leading?

You adorn yourselves with crown of earthly riches.
But the poor have crowns of thorns.
We did the same to our Savior.
We made a fatal mistake when we turned away from Him.

The only reason we are here today is because He showed us grace.
Hear the bays of death.
Investigate your path's direction.
Wear a crown that is everlasting.

For what are we truly doing if we declare that our actions are only beneficial?
Does this then make us liars?
We know that all we do does not benefit others.
Therefore,
What we say would be considered balderdash.

I wonder what lies beneath the facade of perfection.
Is what lies underneath perfection decay?
Is what lies underneath facade hopelessness?

Thinking you'll never be as good as your neighbor.
Thinking you'll always be alone in a crowd.
Forgetting the days you were happy.
Perhaps what lies underneath is something else.

Please don't go deaf now.
Please don't put on blinders.
Please do not elevate your own pedestal.
Please search for the truth.
Please search for the truth because the owners
of the bays can arrive at any time.

<u>Shelter</u>

I need shelter from this weather.
It wears great boulders into pebbles and steadfast oak trees into mere
branches.

Man can build fortresses out of wood to withstand the weather temporarily.
At some point.
The rain eats the wood and collapses the man's fortress.
At this point,
All man can do is stay.
But there will be times that man must fight and stand his ground.
He must fight to stand in his hurricane while I try to keep warm in my blizzard.

The Lamb dances in hurricanes and frolicks in blizzards.

When I invited the Lamb into my home.
The storms did not disappear or lessen.
I wasn't impervious to disaster.

But now.
When the weather comes.

*I don't fear for my life because now I can see the Lamb dancing in the worst
of the storm.*

This is how I know that my body might soon perish.
But my spirit and soul will forever dance with the Lamb.

Prayer

What is the purpose of praying if there is no faith in the one you're
praying to?
In the same ideal.
Why do we cast seeds when the wind is strong?

When we pray,
Or sow to the wind,
We remain fruitless.

But if we wholly trust and know the nature and character of God-
The only true God-
To whom we pray,
Can't I then rest in the assurance that the God that holds everything
in his hands also holds my life?

Now,
When we cast out seed,
We can tell the weather.
We can find and reap the good harvest.

To whom do you pray?
For whom do you sow?

Slow Change

Isn't it odd how change can come slowly?
I would have thought that change is always a split-second action.
What change do you think is most impactful?

I would say that slow change is most important and lasting.

I expected to be shut down or put on hold.
But I was instead met with a strong want to listen and protect.

It has taken many times to hear something that I did not anticipate to
begin to realize that we both long to connect without judgment.
We just both have protective minds.

I can't expect a mother or father such as mine to not protect.
But I can expect them to want a connection.

Words can be misperceived.
It is important to keep relationships that are healthy.
Supportive.
And positive.

Get grace but also give grace.
Grace is the key to all healthy relationships.

The Reality of the "Green Goblin

I cannot be two.
I can't have both evil and innocence.
I am not even good when I am alone in myself.

The Goblin is Satan telling me lies.
The Goblin was me at birth.

Some ask me to realize that I am the Goblin,
But they also say that I am not fully him.

I can't be both.

I can be freed by the Lamb.

When I accept the Lamb,
The Goblin only enters my life when I falter.
He has no power in comparison to the Lamb.
Once the Lamb saves me,
I am a sheep forever.

I am not both good and evil.
Rather,
I have the characteristics of the Lamb and the Goblin.

I was born in the world on sin,
But I have decided to follow in the steps of the Lamb.
I am not perfect.

I am not good.
I am not bad.
The Lamb is the good in me.

Little Row Boat (God's P.O.V.)

Little row boat,
In the middle of the sea.
Come and search for me.
The fog lies thick as the pale moon glows.
The darkness makes it too hard to see.

(So) Send out an S.O.S.
(So) Turn on a light to see.
(So)Yell at the top of your lungs to find me.

Your story isn't done just quite yet.
Your heart hasn't finished its story.
The film hasn't finished its rounds yet.
Keep on.
Keep on and find me.

The waves grow bigger and larger.
The thunder roars more and more.
The birds that circle round you are greedy.
Somehow you're still bored.
How can I answer if your calls are empty?

You turn away to see.
You turn your back to me.
When I walk through your door you are
saying that you are ready.
You say that you have sent our a plea.
You say that you are ready to go.
But you're not truly free.

I wish you would hear my voice.
I wish you could go out for me.
I wish that you could follow me.
But you can't until you're truly free.

(So) Send out an SOS.
(So) Turn on a light to see.
(So)Yell at the top of your lungs to find me.

You're not listening for my voice.
You haven't adopted my heart.
I want your film to run with mine.

Come.

Come find me.

You turn your back and run.

You stand on uneven ground.

You find unhealthy people to run to.

But still look away from me.

I love you much more than they can.

I want to hold onto you tightly.

I want you to break down in my arms,

And find comfort in me.

You sent out your S.O.S.

You turned on your light to see.

You yelled at the top of your lungs to
find me.

Your story is not done just quite yet.

Nor your heart has finished its song.

A new film needs to be wound.

A new song needs to be started.

You finally found me waiting.

You finally found my arms.

I have been waiting forever.

And now you have come.

Now's the Time to go out.

Now's the time to speak .

Share My love with others...

Tell everyone you find.

And give them a chance to see.

When this life is over you will come and live
with me

WHEN THE LIGHTS GO OUT

Are you afraid when the lights go out?

The darkness that closes in on you,
and the creatures that silently stalk you-
Is this not reason enough to run and cower?

Have you heard the crazed laughter or the silent screams in the dark?

I promise that I heard it all too when I visited the darkness.

Once you're accustomed to the dark doesn't it feel rather safe,familiar,and comfortable?

I can assure you that what you feel is a lie.

The horrific things that occur when you've made the dark your home will make you feel lost.

The sun that once shone on you and the friends that made you feel loved...
It seems so far away,
Doesn't it?

I can't get you out of the darkness.
I can't save you from the never satisfied creatures of the dark, but I can tell you who can.

I knew a man before I ventured into the darkness.

He was kind,
Gracious,
Merciful,
Loving,
And so much more.

He was My *all.*

Now,
You may ask why I left him...
To be honest I didn't see what i had...
So I took him for granted.

I can tell you how to find him...

There is a book-
a truthful book-
It tells you his story and why he saved me.

He can save you also...
If you reach out to him and believe and accept the TRUTH.

Would you believe me if I told you that the man who saved me is
the true God's son?

He is unchanging and steadfast.

He can help you get out of the darkness..

The question now is not.
"How do I get out of here?"
The question is.
"Do I want to get out of here?"

FRIENDSHIP

So Long for Now

Graduates and guests.
Lend me your ears.
Now is the time to celebrate.
These people here have succeeded at school.
And they're moving on in life.

Prepare to party.
Prepare to work.
Be prepared to share God's love with everyone.
You'll be sorely missed.
And we'll want you back.
But stand strong in the will of our God.

Here's a secret only y'all can know:
I've been at home so long I'm ready to go.
We're all ready to move on.
But we're not ready to let you go.

Here's a plan I have for you:
It's clear that you are leaving soon.
So I plan for when you return.
To have a great time and to see that through.

Oh.
But must you leave so soon?
It feels like only yesterday I met you.
Here's the things you need to know.

So that when you go.
You won't feel alone.
God is with you.
Deuteronomy.
He'll give you rest in Matthew.
Oh.
Exodus.
He'll fight for you.
He'll guide you through in James.
You're not alone.

Oh.
Life seems so short.
But look back and rejoice.
All the years you spent happily.
Enjoying your time on this earth.
Life seems short to us when we rush around way too much.
So.
Sit back and enjoy this ride.
I cannot come along this time.
But I'll wait for you to come back.

Prepare to party.
Prepare to work.
Be prepared to share God's love with everyone.
You'll be sorely missed.
And we'll want you back.
But stand strong in the will of our God.

SLEEPOVER CRAZE

Stayin' up late with so much to do.
There are crazy new lyrics that have to do
with food.
I think my friends have lost their minds.
But that's okay with me.

Stayin' up late with my friends on my mind.
Music and sleep sound both just fine.
Crazy lyrics comin' to life.
Hush to whispers now.

Laughs that don't make much sense ring on
through the room again
Bobby the pillow needs CPR.
Poor little thing.
Announcing new songs that make no sense.
Up 'till one for no reason.
A new band name.
The Midnight Angels.
Just for fun.
No other reason.

The silks cause harm to those who dared.
The tie-dye shirts are too wet to wear.
Ice cream dreams,
So sweet and good.
The dogs played late 'till they crash and
burn.
The adults sleep so unaware of the crazy
things we dare to do.
The strange new songs and the sweet new
tunes.
We're having sleepover crazies.

Stayin' up late with my friends on my mind.
Music and sleep sound both just fine.
Crazy lyrics comin' to life.
Hush to whispers now.
Hush to whispers now.

A FLIGHT WORTH FLYING

Fly away from here.
Find a different path.
Find a cliff and jump.
Then spread your wings.

Soar above the ground.
And never look down.
Look on to the light ahead.

Find a real good friend.
And help each other out.
Find the rock to cover you in the rain.

Care to make amends.
And love 'em to the end.
Who knows when someone will need a hand?

Please.
Find the right path.
Find the sun now.
Don't stop now.
Keep going 'till the end.
Fix the broken.
And sing His song again.

Fear will strike you fast when you're runnin' from the sun.
Shadows haunt your mind.

Now, it's time to fight back.
Stand your ground and overcome your fears.

Please.
Find the right path.
Find the sun now.
Don't stop now.
Keep going 'till the end.
Fix the broken.
And sing His song again.

Remembering a Friend

The feeling came fast towards my brain.
It overwhelmed and satisfied my pain.
She's leaving now.
And it won't be the same.
It won't be the same.

I wish she wouldn't go.
But she must.
She loves it there much more than anywhere else.

The things that I never did do with her:
I never got to paint in a coffee shop.
I never got to show her both of my dogs.
We never went on a walk down the street.
We never hung out whenever we pleased.
I missed out.
I missed out on so many things.

When will she return?
Who knows?
She's got some family here.
So that's a rope to my home.
I wanted to tell her to stay.

She is radiant as a light in the black sky.
She is a diamond in the rough.
She is an answered prayer.

I won't erase the memories of you.
I won't forget your kindness,
Nor your truths.
I want to thank you for what you've given me.

I hope that she writes from time to time.
I hope that her smile stays the same.
I hope that she knows that she is missed.

But she's probably in the mountains,
Or in a field with some friends.
She's probably painting under a vast open sky.
She's probably shining her light so brightly.

Held

Thank you for holding me in a way that I've never been held.

Kept Safe

Thank you for keeping me safe from myself.

<u>Response to Post</u>

Pictures in red and black.

Standing on granite.
A reflection stares.
Only one smile shows through.

It takes work to smile.

Post.

Guy with music in his world responds to give hope.

Don't worry. You gotta go through bad before you get to the good.

Hours later.
A story appears with an identical message.

He tries.
No.
He shines.

Will I accept?

Will I endure?

One way or another.
Everything will be okay.

Will it?

Do I want it to?

Hope from a friend who shines so bright.

A friend.

A friend.

THE ACCOUNT

My account of the situation
is most likely different than
yours.

I saw violence without a
cause.
I heard cursing out of the
blue.
I experienced a cold
countenance from an old
friend.

You might've seen a friend
defending a victim of
harassment.
You might've seen someone
cursing at life.
You might've seen an old
friend suffering from the
world's cruelty.

We might not agree on the
action of response.
We might not agree on how
the situation went down.

*The only true thing is that we
might have different
accounts.*

Everything but Nothing

Two hands.
I only have two hands.

Something that was intended to be sweet was kind.
But I could tell that it was tense.
Even so,
I chose to be grateful.

My ears burned cold when my heart began to race.

Prisoners to evil.
Prisoners of the world.
Prisoners to corruption.
Unassuming people fall prey to the lies of this world.
Knowledgeable people fall prey to the lies of this world.

Money.
Money is how to help.

Really though?

What about prayer?

What about not being a predator?

What would've happened if ice cream with him was my downfall?

Would it have been once or more?

How many people fall prey to his sickeningly sweet words?

Who are you truly?

Is it not enough to supply the sweet after disappointment?

Does it do nothing when I try to make my life easier?

Why am I constantly the prey?

I've wasted away my day with the changes.
I've taken care of life and seen God's creatures at ease.
In result,
I'm told that to do one's responsibilities.

The one who I once butted heads with cares.
God hears my cries.
The Creator cares.

I wasn't told the circumstances that aided the chaos.
They didn't even try to tell me.

Why lie to save your reputation when I have no one left?

I don't know your story.
But you do not know mine.

BELONGING

Welcome

Welcome to our church.
Welcome to our family of love.
Our arms are open wide.
And our hearts soar above the skies.
Welcome to our church.

Love.
Love is like a wildfire spreading like a flood.
God's love is never-ending.
Hope.
Hope is like a storm.
Coming in and washin' 'way the doubt.
Joy.
Joy is a celebration coming through us now.
Rejoice.

Welcome to our church.
Welcome to our family of love.
Our arms are open wide.
And our hearts soar above the skies.
Welcome to our church.

Life.
The twisting turning path.
There's light among the wrath.
So wait with hope until tomorrow.

Faith.

Faith is something fierce.
It's something to hold on to.
So.
Hold on to it tight 'till tomorrow.

First.
I need to tell you something.
Something that is fun.
Our energy never ends at all.
Now.
I need to tell you something.
Something you should know.
Sometimes we're like siblings.
Bicker to and fro.

Welcome to our church.
Welcome to our family of love.
Our arms are open wide.
And our hearts soar above the skies.
Welcome to our church.

Welcome (Part Two)

Welcome to our church.
Welcome to our family of love.
Our arms are open wide,
And our hearts soar above the skies.
Welcome to our church.

A year has passed since you first came 'round.
How's it here now that you're on the ground?
Do you remember all the fun we had just last year?

We planned a barbeque but didn't go through.
We went to the beach and got sand everywhere.
Christmas came 'round,
And your kids got a gift.
Notes rang through the air.
The white elephant at youth group was long.
The gifts were strange,
But that made it fun.
We kayaked through the mangrove tangle and lost some members
in the maze you trampled.
Yeah.
Mike fell out,
But he won't say.
Take my word when I say he did.
We went on a boat,
But the waves were too rough.
We ended up at the beach instead.

UNCOVERING

HOPE

Coming Together ('Cause Covid)

There's a sickness here.
And it's so feared.
People stay away.
They stay out of my way.

I walk into a store,
And people look at me with fear.
My eyes go to the floor because I am not afraid of this.

Yes,
Many people are dying,
And people are losing their friends.
But I am not afraid of this because God has a plan.
Still,
People are dying left and right,
And many are full of grief and strife.

But people are coming together.
They're connecting with old friends and new.

I know that terrible things are going on.
But I can't help but sing.

Yes,
People are coming together.
They're connecting with old friends and new.
They're supporting one another with confidence and love.
Yes,

People are coming together.
They're uplifting one another.

It is true that people are dying,
And people are losing their jobs.
But I know that one thing is for certain:
God's watching over us.

Terrible things are happening right now.
And I can't say they're nothing.
I also know that God is in control,
And I have nothing to fear.

Odd

Isn't it odd when tears come forth because of someone?

Isn't it odd when the source of tears comes from unexpected places?

Isn't it odd when the person you butt heads with the most says something so meaning and moving that tears dream down your cheeks?

Isn't it odd when the same person you once saw as a frightening neighbor now recognizes and adopts God's forgiveness and adopts his grace?

Isn't it odd that this person will be who gives you tough love,
Truth,
And a shove in the direction of your potential?

Isn't it odd that when forgiveness is given,
The clouds finally move,
And the sun shines through.

Aren't a lot of things odd when you think about it?

Fly

I must spread my broken wings and try to fly.

<u>Plant</u>

I plant flowers,
But I grow weeds:
Beautiful & ugly.

Wishes into Dreams

I want to go home,
Where the streets are rolling gold.
I want to go home,
Where His arms are open wide.
I see my future with happiness inside.
Why won't it come close?
Why does it want to hide?

Hope,
I called your name aloud.
I sang it from the mountains.
You came a little late,
But that's okay.

I held on with the last of my strength.
I held my own in the rush of the waves.
I found the ones who could stand by me bravely.
My fight is not done today.

Hope,
I called your name aloud.
I sang it from the mountains.
You came a little late,
But that's okay.
I'm okay.

Oddly Beautiful

The rain's been falling for so long.
The clouds cover the sun.
The lightning strikes.
The thunder booms.
The rain falls hard.

Now it is night.
And it still goes on.
The rain keeps coming.

The families gather and play some games.
Bonding is coming strong.

The thunder booms among the night.
And the lightning flashes before my eyes.

The symphony is playing.

Rain still falls.
The lightning strikes.
The thunder booms among the night.

The symphony is playing.

Leaving Behind the Lies

Every moment is a waking dream.
Every second is shorter than it seems.

I've found a way to follow you.
But then I lost sight of myself.

You left.
And I followed all the way 'till tomorrow.
You closed me out.
But I still stood.

I waited.
You promised to stand here through the darkness and the light.

You said that I could not lose you that easy.

But you left me easily.
You left so quickly.
You left so harshly.

When I woke up.
I searched for you.

But now I am finding who I truly am when I take you out of my plans.

What I could...
No.
What I can yet be.

I am finding the blessings laid for me.

They were always here in front of me.
But I have been blind.
I have been blind though their light shone.
And everyone else saw.
It was.
It is God's light.

Well.
I was blind until you left.
Now I see what lies before me.
Now I can see the ones to lean on.
Now I know who to truly seek.
I know who to love fully and fear equally.

You left me in the ash.
But like a phoenix with its task I rose above myself and served the superior one.

I want to serve God wholeheartedly.
I give myself to Him.

I falter.
I stumble.
I cannot fly on my own.
So He helps me up.
And I show him off to my town.
To my friends.
To my family.
And to my heart.

Breathe

Yeah.
Sometimes it is hard to breathe.

I was drowning, breaking, dying when God opened my eyes, My story can help others, but it can also help me, Reach out... Reach out to find ME, I didn't understand until an amber sent by God suggested it, I thought that my story I was fine... that it is, Hear, wasn't for me, but ME my child, You Come back to ME off... you're MINE, Can't Shake ME I walked lost for a I'm God's, but HE drew me back, It bit, truly took a how to reel me back, but I'm glad HE did, I'm back, back where I belong... and if I ever get lost again I want HIM to draw me back, no matter how HE does it, I'm thankful for the friends who stood by me in My low, For those who supported me, Because Some were only for a season but I'll remember them, They truly impacted my life... and I'm so glad that I was given those moments because they're now a part of my story...

MY RECOVERY

I was drowning.
Breaking.
Dying when God opened my eyes.

My story can help others.
But it can also help me.

                                              Reach out.
                                              Reach out.
                                    Reach out to find ME.

I didn't understand until an amber sent by God suggested it.

I thought that I was fine...
That my story wasn't for me.
But it is.

                                                   Hear.
                                       Come back to ME.
                                               My child.

                                    You can't shake ME off...
                                          You are MINE.

I am God's.

I walked lost for a bit,
But HE drew me back.

It truly took a low to reel me back,

But I'm glad HE did.

I'm back.
Back where I belong......
And if I ever get lost again,
I want HIM to draw me back in any way HE chooses.

I'm thankful for the friends who stood by me in my low,
And for those who supported me...
Even though some were only for a season,
I'll remember their kindness...
Because they truly impacted my life...
And I am so glad that I was given those moments because they're
now a part of my story...
MY RECOVERY

Stars

There is light in the darkness.
Specks of light float inside my darkness.

There is light in the darkness.
These are called stars.

Memories and friends are stars.

Fighting and depression are black holes.

Which will win?

Will I win and see every day?

No Worries

It's not possible to be worry-free.
I wish it were.
But it simply cannot be.

If we had no worries,
Then what would life be?
A life on endless repeat with no changes-
That's life worry-free.
If there were changes,
We would worry.

Is this the life we yearn for?

Why be worry-free if we can just be?

Just live.
Just deal with life as it comes.
That is the kind of life I want.

How is yours going to be?

Let's both be free to experience and learn how to LIVE.

Run

Run.
I dare you to run.
There might be a ton of trouble ahead,
But right now,
The hell on earth is overwhelming.

The sun may be hot.
The terrain may be mysterious.
But when a friend is forced to leave,
I can't stay in that hell.

The tall shrubbery of trees and grass lured me to the safety of
coverage.
The short fields and tall fields of corn hid me from men.

The thirst and heat attacked my throat.

RUN.

I can't escape this hell,
But I can try.

ExtraOrdinary

I think that snow is extraordinary.

Before you can say that snow is common.
Let me say that I live in Florida.

To me.
Snow falling looks like rain falling in slow motion.
I haven't seen rainfall in slow motion.
And I doubt that I ever will.
But that doesn't change my wonderment about snow.

Seeing snow fall slowly and continuously is amazing.
It's amazing to see how quickly snow builds into drifts.
It makes me wonder how much sand exists.

I thought sand was a monotonous commonality.
But now.
I am trying to open my eyes wider for the extraordinary in the ordinary.

Earthquake

Hearing the song of a guitar again makes me yearn to learn the song hidden in me.

An earthquake of music has shifted my soil.
Will new plants grow,
Or will the soil dry?
I want to learn,
But I'm embarrassed to ask.

I have nothing else to lose.
I'm going to take the risk.
I want to find my song.

First Day On

Time is an oxymoron:
It's fast and slow.

The first interactions were definitely hard.
I was a new gear in a well-working machine.

I was an observer...
Until I was not.

Standing wasn't a task so serious.
Until I needed to.

I'm a working gear.

I'm a part of the machine,
But I'm not at the same pace as the others.

First day on.
But it feels so long.

I s'pose gears never stop turning.

The Blackened Rose

A blood-red rose stands out amongst the flowers.

Her leaves dance gracefully in the wind.
Some of her leaves are ruined with wear and some grow strong.

She was born into the world with delicate leaves.
Her petals were marbled gray and white.
Her thorns used to keep the weeds and predators away.

She loved to watch the bees because they were fluffy and pretty.
But she learned that bees were also intelligent and hard-working.

The rose loved to gossip with her family about the flowers that only came around in the summer.

As time passed.
The rose's friends and family left her.
One by one her friends went with huge creatures to a new home.

Her petals turned red with bitterness as she thought about her family...
Even though they were overjoyed to be loved she knew they were discarded and forgotten about later.

The rose wondered why all of her family wanted to leave their home.

One day she finally asked one of her family members why he wanted to leave.

He said,
"I will be used to bring people together. If I stay here I will get old and wither, but if I bring people together when I have the chance before I die my life will not end uselessly."
After he said this the rose understood.

She was filled with a new purpose.
And she shed her petals turned back into a marbled white and gray.

She was filled with new hope and joy.
She finally realized that her life could have purpose in another's life.

J.A.S.P.E.R.

Change brings its own kind of chaos.
But aside from that the day was J.A.S.P.E.R.

It was *Just Astounding* in the sense that the day was lovely.
Today it was warm with a slight breeze.

It was *Spectacular* because sternness softened to kindness.

It was *Peaceful* because no major drama occurred.

It was *Earnest* because honesty and reflection sank into dear relationships.

It was *Real* because the words and emotions were true.

I'm going to try to make tomorrow J.A.S.P.E.R. too.

Wonderland

Ludicrous,
the rabbit is never late,
The queen has a violent tendency,
The Hatter is insane and unstable,
And food is dangerously magical.

Sadly,
Nothing exciting happens here.

So tell me,
Why we call home "wonderland".

Home is not wonderful...Not anymore.

Wonderland was once unique,
At the start,
But now everything is normal.

I'm not even considered eccentric.

We have not ever changed...
Can we?

I yearn for some new wonderful chaos,
For the thrill of something new in this world,
For a catalyst to inspire some change,
But that won't happen naturally.

I will make a portal.

I will force some change.

I will bring in a new variable..

A creature from another world will bring all in Wonderland to an insane change.

Obviously.
I am the most insane.

~the Cheshire Cat

LOVE

Underneath

There's something darker underneath;
Darker than I've ever witnessed.

Love and Law

I want it...
But it's wrong.
Why must it be this way?

Love, Halt

It's what I want.
But not this way.
Definitely not this way.

Uncertainty

I still don't know how I feel about you.
About this.
About everything.

Unhealthy Hugs

I miss hugs.
I remember your hug.
I crave more.

Lonely

I'm scared that I won't find a lover.
I'm scared that I won't find a partner.
I'm scared that I won't find a mate.
Nobody loves me like that.

I long for someone to intimately love me as my partner.

What if I have no shoulder to lay on when I return home from work?
What if I still lie in my room wondering how much easier life could be with another?
What if I'm the only one in my friend group that no guy looks at twice?
What if I can't fully understand "LOVE" because I've never felt it as strong as one in a relationship?

The Note

I wrote a list of guided questions on the backside of a paper.
I asked a friend to pass it down.
And they did so down the row.
I saw a friend grab a pen and hand it to my target.
He then returned to his girlfriend.
I got my note back and saw a lot of yeses.
The three questions were all answered with a yes.
A question was answered...
Now what?

Enclosed

I've enclosed my feelings.
My wants.
And my desires in this gray envelope.
I want to send this letter.

I want to publicize my feelings for you.
But an external force hinders me from doing so.

I fear being caught and separated if I leave the letter addressed
and out for you.

Of course I'm afraid that you will receive my letter and be surprised
in all the wrong ways.
But at least my breath wouldn't be full with words that need to be
released.

Alone

I used to feel alone.
As if I could find a mate for myself.

I saw my friends find mates of their own.
While I was on the sidelines.
They leaned on their partner in times that all seemed hopeless.

There are instances when only one's mate can console a person.

I wonder if my partner will love or use me.
I've only been played with in the past.

Love seems to be too good to be true.

I know that partners at a younger age may fade.
Even so.
It is my longing.

I don't want to be without a mate.
I don't want to be alone.

<u>Pause. Not Stop</u>

Waiting isn't a rejection.
That is what he said.

He doesn't want to hurt me.
And for that.
I am grateful.
But I cannot help but worry that I spoke too soon and wrongly.

I usually keep my mouth shut and do not hand out my letters.
The result is me regretting and forgetting.

We both know what I want:
A relationship that will not cease.

Now I do still want that.
But I can wait for a second more.

But I can't wait forever.
Please don't make me wait forever.
Because I do not want to be alone.

A Strong Yearning

I've never felt as alone as I do now.

My friends spit venom at me and watch me shatter.
I wish you were here with me.
If you were here,
You'd shelter me from their words.

Your presence allows me to break when I can't be whole.
I know that your love will envelope me.
You will shield my broken pieces from the wind.
Your eyes hold a love that I have not yet see.

I want you to be mine.
Perhaps I want you too much.

I hope it is me you love and want.
I want to be your everything.

Make your home with me.
I'll love and support you.
I'll stay with you through hell and high water.
I'll make sure you don't walk this life alone.

MELANCHOLY/ANGER

The Inner Battle

Here I am.
I'm sitting on the floor all alone again.
I'm waiting for something to happen.
I'm staring at the screen that looks back at me.

Here I am.
I'm waiting on the floor with some friends.
I see them way too often.
They wade through my mind with some lies.

Here I am.
I stand on the battlefield of lies.
I stand here while the other cries.
I stand here with guilt.
But I cannot move to save.

Here I stay.
To move on would be brave.
But the fear that holds me here makes me feel welcome.

Now it comes.
A light unto another road.
And a voice to lead me home.

Should I go?
Should I go?

I click on the mic and turn on my smile.

It's time to go out and be brave.

Another night left,
And a new day has come.
It's time to go on.

I can't stop.
I can't stop from blocking everything out.
I can't stop.
I can't stop to say *amen*.
I can't stop from being tired.
I can't stop the acts because they're all wired.

Here I stand.
I stand on the battlefield of lies.
I stand here while the other cries.
I stand here with guilt,
But cannot move to save.

Now it comes,
A light unto another road,
And a voice to lead me home.

Should I go?
Should I go?

A Brief Word

I write a thousand songs about the world when it's gone.
While all I want to do is fade away.
I've held on for so long.
Now I cannot see the sun.
When I see a light,
I close my eyes.

Push On

I see her light in front of me.
It shines with the brightest purity.
With her hands in her hair.
She swears at the sky above.

She has a broken family.
One that's whole but not in peace.
She can't see the light that surrounds her life.
The light that conquers the darkest night.

She hides behind a mask and takes it off when she's to sleep.
She cannot lend her trust to anyone to keep.

She wallows in sorrow too paralyzed to move.
She's unable to go forward.
And the darkness grins ahead.

She won't give in just yet.
Too many people care.
The only one opposed is her own self.
Who cares?

She hides behind a mask and takes it off when she's to sleep.
She cannot lend her trust to anyone to keep.

The night continues on.
And the sun is so close to peek.
She cannot give a damn about what anybody thinks.

The Door

I reside behind a closed door some say to leave ajar.
But if I leave it open.
The devil dances in.

When it's sealed.
I am safe.
And shadows only linger.
The shades are drawn.
And light's about outside.

The darkness's caressing figure.
The drumming of my heart can be erratic or on beat.
Nothing really matters.
Well.
That's what it seems.

The cruelness of this world is misconceived by most.
But I perceive the world for what it truly is:
Deceiving and a hoax.

Someday.
When life has exceeded its limit and serenity is bountiful in the sea.
Nothing that is malevolent will be able to locate me.

Black Hole

A massive bottomless vacuum opens underneath my feet.
Only my shoestrings are victims of its group.

As I run my race time after time,
My hopefulness undulates just as the breeze.
But with passing fights to the finish,
My endurance will begin to deplete.

My feet and then legs enter the pit.

People don't want to hold you.
It's enough for them to enjoy life as it is.
Sinking beneath all else rids them of time that might've been wasted.

My chest is soon out of sight in the entrancing doom.

Pressure and disappointment weigh heavy as a stone,
Forcing me to be devoured into my fate...
But not too quick though.

Life, A Dream?

Why does life feel like a dream?
That if I die,
I'll wake up from a nightmare.

If I knew life was a dream,
I'd kill myself.
No need to endure unnecessary torture.

If life were a dream,
What would I wake to be?

If life were a dream,
What would I find when I wake?

If life is real,
Then why?

If life is real,
Why must I continue?

If life is real,
I want to know why I must endure this punishment.

If life is real,
Let mine end.

When? Why? Still?

When is the world-changing moment,
The one that is awaited?
When will my soul no longer cry?
When will my heart no longer lie?
When will I be free of the earth's pull?
When will my vision halt?
When will my mind rest?
When will I no longer have to worry about things?
When will my chest stop hurting,
As it does so often.

When?

When?

Why??

Why does repopulation occur?
Why do we create more to be destroyed?
Why do we make generations to punish them?
Why can't we hit an end button?

Still.

Still,
One day it'll end.
Still,
One day my body and breath will be.

Still,
Will be my hope.

Sixteen Years

I'm in fifteen years.
Fourteen years accomplished.
Fifteen so close.
Yet so far to finish.
If the time comes...

How do you celebrate sixteen years if you aren't too excited to live sixteen years?

Seventeen too far to think.
Fifteen still in progress.
Sixteen years.

Let the celebration for sixteen years occur
(You can handle that preparation).
I'll just focus on making my goal.

Empty

I just feel empty.
As if there is an endless vacuum in my entire being.
I feel like there is nothing propelling me forward except for a slight breeze.
I feel like I am being swallowed by what captured me last summer.
I feel like I have to fight to breathe.
I feel like this battle is near its end.
I feel that my fight is weakening.
I feel like I want to cry but cannot.
I am exhausted.
I can't talk to anyone.
For everything around me is moving.

I don't know how much more I can endure.
Let me be devoured by the darkness.
If you want to save me.
Make sure you understand the battle.
If you want to save me,
Fight with me.
If you want to save me,
"Help."

Selfish

I'm selfish.
I want to hit the accelerator.
I want to jerk the wheel to a side and deal with the consequences.
I want to swallow the pills and feel the pain.
I want to say "goodbye."
But I can't.

I can't.
I can't.
I can't.

I have to see tomorrow.
I have to because there must be something better.
There has to be.
There has to be.
Please.

Emotions Amass

How do I abandon anxiety,
And why won't it ever abate?
I can make an abatis with my trees of progress,
But anxiety advances as if my abatis were a red carpet.
With anxiety comes stress.
They cannot camouflage themselves when they're afar because they
cause my brain to run amok.
I don't know how to appease them,
And I don't know how to be free.
All I know is how to save them for a later date.

While anxiety and stress lurk in the shadows,
Loneliness sneaks up from behind.
Once it has me in its sights,
It's nearly impossible to evade.
Loneliness obscures my vision and keeps me captive while doubt
swoops in.
Doubt seizes control of my mind.
That's when anxiety and stress make their move.
All of the feelings pile on top of me and weigh me to the ground.
I alone can't do anything to make these invisible beasts retreat,
But I can ask people to help drive them away.

Makeup

There was a time in my life when I didn't understand makeup.
I didn't understand why someone would take minutes of their day and later undo that work.

I understand as I watch my reflection.
I understand as I apply the makeup.

I build up my wall.
I feel a bit safer behind the wall.
Only some can see through this wall is meant to fool the surface.

The true people will see me.
I will wear my makeup.
Days by days will pass 'til one day the makeup will lay lonely on the counter.

Haze

I started today asleep.
The world closed before the sun arose.
Today was a strange day because disassociation was at play.

A Friday that ended as soon as it began.
The car skidding.
Slipping.
Near to hitting.
But reigned control too soon.

My selfish wish was almost fulfilled.
What if it did?
I wouldn't be here.

A car and a rained road by chance.
A week was finished.
And a new to begin.
Oh goodness.
Let's go before I think.

Another week.
Another day.
One more.
One more.
One more.

My Brittle Promise

I know that it's wrong to miss you as much as I do,
But I long for the lingering pain that reminds me you're here.

I've tried to walk away from you.
I've tried to leave you behind.
Is it possible to be completely rid of you?

I miss the calm and anxiety you bring.
I miss the ever growing pride because of your presence.
I momentarily felt the pride after you left,
But now it's mostly gone.

I was addicted to having you around.
I know I said that I left you behind,
But now I struggle to keep the promise I made to myself.

ReEncounter

As I've said before,
I've missed your presence.

I brought you back today to remember how I felt with you here.

When you arrived,
It hurt as bad as I remember,
But the satisfaction and pleasure weren't as I recalled.

Perhaps it's because you didn't bring your stinging words.
I kinda wonder how our reencounter would've gone if you were like that.

How I remember you was not the same as today.
I don't know if I should dare to meet with you again,
For I fear that I will become addicted to your unhealthy habits.
I long to experience your bite again.

Should I?
No.
But parts of me longs for your presence.

I recognized you were different than I recalled.
Your facade is now shattered.
You're now prohibited from my mind.

I can break down your deceiving facades now.

Panic in the Car

I feel panic.

Pure panic ripping through my chest.

I hear my thoughts.

Why won't you kill yourself?
Because of the pain?
You don't feel much of anything.
So what's bad with this?
At least you'll have a chance at dying.

I am shaking.

I can't stop.

I'm scared.

I am so scared.

I have the supplies.

I have the means.

But I can't.

I can't allow myself to.

I'm scared.

Even if I made it through this,
I'll have to fight it again.

I'm scared.

I'm scared.

I'm scared.

Hear the Music

I want to hear the music.
But the amp is slowly dying.

I want to play my song.
But my fingers are bleeding.
I want to put on an honest show.
But the cables of lies are twisted.

How will I play and put on my show?
I do not honestly know.

My fans are restless and quickly disappointed.

My parent's fights sing louder than anything I can play.
Only one thing is louder than fights...
Silence.

The silence that makes people weep is louder than fights.
I hope I don't get close to that silence again.

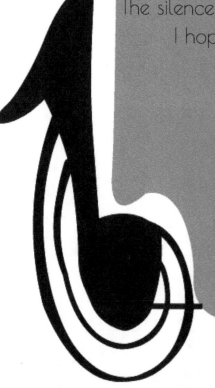

Shatter Me

It's not hard to shatter me.
All it takes is a touch or a word.

Why can't I be myself in public?
Why can't I have fun amongst the crowd?

Am I so much that you feel that you must shut me down?

I wish I were impervious to your harshness.
But I'm not.

Every time you stop me from being myself,
I feel a piece of me weaken.

You fickle-minded people tell me to be myself.
But when I am myself,
You shut me down.

You keep breaking me.
You shatter my broken pieces.

Don't you dare try to console me when you're holding the hammer.

If you're going to shatter me, do so, but don't leave.

I can't break into smaller pieces than I already have.

Break me more than I am now and see what happens.
If you're going to break me,
I dare you to stay and see what happens.

Drown

Just let me drown.

I'm already neck-deep in others' scorns.
I've reached the point of insanity.
I feel like laughing out loud.
I'm so hurt that I just want to laugh and cry.

Let me inhale the hurt and drown beneath the words.
The world's crap has passed the point of overwhelming.
Peoples' words no longer sting.

I have so many deep cuts in my being.
They're as visible as the cuts I put on myself.

You've poured gallons upon gallons of water on me.
But for some reason you don't think it's enough.
If you're going to pour gallons of water on me,
Just let me drown.

Don't drown me and then try to save me.
Make your choice.
Drown me or let me be.

Story

For each cut is a story:
Some are lonely.
Some are painful.
Some are hopeless.
I gain numerous stories over time.

Scars are a story,
And my body is a canvas.
No matter if it is ink,
Or scar,
Or an invisible mark,
There is a story.
Some can read the story,
And some can't.

Are you going to read the stories or skim them?

Under Ice

My lungs burned with fire from my sprint,
But now they burn with the loss of warmth.

The frigid water calls my name.
I answer its call with eager feet.

The water's cold is a comforting change,
But there is a thick layer of ice above me.
I can't bring myself to fight the ice.
I can't breach the surface again,
So I dive deeper.

I hear a splash behind me,
But I continue to swim down.
The tendrils of the dark water lead me to the soft sand at the bottom
of the lake.

Cold water fills my stomach,
My nose burns,
And my lungs shriek,
But I don't swim for the surface.

Some people say that before you die,
You see your life flash before your eyes.
All I see is the murky water before me.
Everything is black, but I know my eyes are open.

Something grabs my wrist and drags me out of the water.

Faint bells ring in my head.
And my lungs become still as the air around me.

Unfair

I wish she wouldn't snap at me when I wasn't the person who drove her anger higher.

I wish I wasn't in this position:
One of isolation within a group and a target on one's back.

I often wish I could run until my breath is ragged.
To where?
Anywhere.
I am currently prohibited from the actualization of such freedom.

I want to vanish into the tall rows of corn.
The rows of corn tower above my height.
But the thought of being alone in the maze is not frightening.
Rather.
Being alone in the corn is exhilarating.

I don't want to have this innocent-looking facade.
But I'm human.
I get hurt too.

Some Memories Don't Fade

Memory has never been one of my best qualities.

What was yesterday except for the words that were written?
I can't remember how old I was in a memory.
Memory is nothing but the past...

I remember how my family has always been a family.
But the memories that easily stick are traumatic.

I've heard that traumas never go away.
I've heard that they don't get easier to battle.
I've heard that I'll be stronger despite trauma.

I'll always remember the loss of Ashley.
I'll remember how unhealthy our relationship was.
I'll remember how she was an anchor in my time of need.

I'll always feel the loss of Matthew's parents.
His father was fired and untruthful to me.
He was a support to his son in the end.
His mother left in pride and deceit.
She supported her son in the end.

I'll always feel the shame of sending him pictures of myself because I
thought I liked him.
The pictures were always clean.
But he still played on my feelings.

I'll always worry about what would've happened if I met him alone.

I'll always remember the guilt he dumped on me because of the texts I shared.
How I was the one who ruined his whole career.
How I was the one who ruined his life.

I'll always remember Ethan's vaping and alcoholic words.
His words were flattering.
And his attention was unhealthy.
The fact that he had a girlfriend and still flirted with me was wrong.

I'll remember the shame of pretending to fall asleep to see his reaction.

I'll remember talking to him for too long about "sticking around" even though I knew it was wrong.

There was good:
I found my true friends and support.
I learned how to set my boundaries.

There is good.
But let me feel the hurt.

The hurt that I will have my entire life.

Do You Want to Know

Do you want to know?
Do you want to see the damage you've done?

You stole a piece of me when I was down.
You took all of my dreams and ran in the opposite direction.
You stole my one and only anchor.

I see how people like you are:
You steal and ravage towns.
You leave ghosts of hope behind you.

I see what people like me are:
We stand up only to be crushed and thrown away.

Did you know that I'm not done?
I'm here right now.
I'm here forever.
So you should run.

I can feel my own wrath.
I'm not weak enough to break.
I will stand in what I know.
Nothing will capsize my boat.

You still try to come at me with your words and vicious thoughts.

I might bruise and break,
But I will never fold.

Watch me roar.
Watch me stand up and not give up hope.

                              I see how people like you are:
                                  You steal and ravage towns.
                          You leave ghosts of hope behind you.

I see what people like me are:
We stand up only to be crushed and thrown away.

People will always stand and judge me.
I will always be susceptible to bruises.
And I may break.
But I'm still here.

I still have my flaws.
I still have my strength.
I still have a cause.

                              I see how people like you are:
                                  You steal and ravage towns.
                          You leave ghosts of hope behind you.

I see what people like me are:
We stand up only to be crushed and thrown away.

The World's People

A lot of people are way too hopeless in life.
There's too many silent depressed people on this planet.
Why is everyone so depressed in the world?

Fade Out

You just took my door...
And now it's taking me my all not to kill myself.
To not OD.
To not run away.

I just want to die.

Please.
Just let me fade away.
Let my life force fade.
Please God.

Please.

Please.

Please.
Let me die.
Lei me be run over
Let me meet my fatality.

I want to end...
Not just this chapter...
This story.
I want my story to end.

Let me FADE OUT.

Here Again

Here we are again...
Will I choose help?

<u>Breathe</u>

Breathe...
But fear shooting through me

<u>Thoughts</u>

I can't speak.
But my thoughts are running rampant.
It's all too much...
Too many...
Soo many thoughts.
I feel the fear spiking through my arms...
My body.
I need to get out of here.
She's crying.
Get me out of here!
Numb
I'm close to numb.
I feel.
But I don't feel.
I care.
But I don't care.
This numbness is strange...
Yet,
I sorta like this.

Speechless
I don't know that I have words for this except that I feel empty and
hurt...
My arm hurts but my inside is empty.

Push

It doesn't take much to dive me over the edge anymore.
I'm already on the edge...
But will you push me off the cliff?
Please.
Push me off the edge.
I'm ready to go.
PUSH ME HARD.

Where to Go

No.
I don't want to go back to the house.
But I can't go anywhere else.
I can't find anywhere else to go.
Please let me end.

Remember

Oh goodness,
I remember stress again:
The shaking in your bones & the fear in your heart.

My Story

Yes,
I've got scars...
They're my story.
Thanks to those who hold my stories and me.

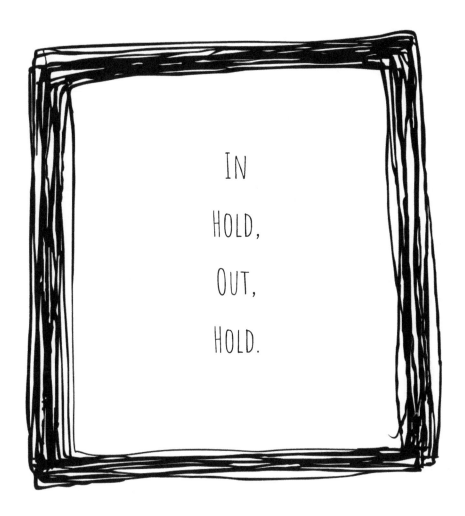

In

Hold,

Out,

Hold.

What to do

I don't want to cut anymore,
But I do.

I use an innocent razor to lightly cut.

Deep or shallow,
A cut is a cut...
And I am cutting.

I know it's wrong,
But it's so satisfying:
The blade,
the pain,
And then the stinging.
It's what I yearn for.

I don't know how to stop.

Should I stop?

Should I stop myself from cutting?

Lost You

I lost you,
And I lost a piece of myself:

My innocence & a piece of love.

Invisible

Some wish to be invisible,
To not be seen by the world.
Some wish to melt into the shadows,
And erase their own mistakes.
I wish to be invisible,
But no one can tell you so;
Because I will deny my insecurities and call out yours instead.

Safely unsafe

Will he tell about my razor?
Or am I safe?

Am I really safe with it?

I think I am.

I don't think I'll cut to kill.

I think I'm safe.

<u>Messed Up</u>

I messed up.

Again and again,
I did it.

                                    The addictive sting came.

Again and again,
I welcomed the pain:
Shallow yet painful.

                                    The cuts appear.

Scarring won't be worrisome,
But I'll know...

I'll know.

                                    Phantom pains.

Phantom memories of stinging.

Feel

I can't feel most anything...
Only pain.

Only pain.
Is what I feel.

BIRTHDAY

It's Your Birthday

I heard it's your birthday today of all the days.

How's it feel to be one year older?

You're wiser than yesterday.

Was your year full of pain and sorrow?

Was your year full of gladness?

It really doesn't matter as long as you're with God.

This year you should set a goal.

Plan to prosper in God's love.

Plan to help people smile.

But don't go too fast.

You'll miss all the blessings and all the fun times that last.

But let's reel back to the reason these words started.

Happy birthday to you {insert name}.

And enjoy today.

It's Your Birthday (Remastered)

I hear it's your birthday today of all the days.
How's it feel to be one year older?
You're wiser than yesterday.
Was your year full of gladness?
Did you laugh at all the jokes?
Can I please have a smile now?
No.
This ain't a hoax.
Happy birthday to you {insert name}.
Happy birthday to you.
Have fun getting older now.
Lots of time to lose.

SCHOOL EVENTS

Race Day at Holloway

Pain in my legs as the morning began.
Mosquitos scouted the course.
Twists and turns forever,
It seemed.
Hills undulating,
Mimicking the waves.
The race began with a second's notice,
Only enough time to pray.
I ran with a teammate ahead of me.
I passed two before the end.
A long stride fell short.
Pain rose,
Shortening my stride.
Gray caught up and I was passed,
But pride is still in me.
My breath fell short and,
My legs burned numbly.
I crossed the raised black line.
The race began and ended forever.
Time seemed everlasting but short.
The canopy of trees stared down at me when I wearily ran.
My knees burned and changed my pace to one much quicker than
the last.
Ending the race was a second best.
Not too bad for me.

Holloway Headache

Pounding.
Pounding.
Pounding.
My head felt like a bomb.
It hurt.
It hurt.
It grew and grew.
After a race pain can ensure.
But it's worth every second:
Every second.
Every minute.
Each step.
I work.
I work towards a goal.
I work to finish my best.

Holloway's Heat

In the heat of the afternoon,
We warmed up for a run.
The exciting long week of school was fun.

Holloway.
Holloway.
We hath meet again.

Holloway.
Holloway,
Once more.
And then again.

Our gun went off as the guys came on in.

Here we go.
Here we go,
Go running yet again.

The first mile was hard,
And the second was the same.
When the third mile came,
Tiredness was calling my name.

Stopping only four times and passing the finish,
Another Holloway race was finished.
Once more,
My energy diminished.

After the race,
I bought a marble shirt.
After the race,
We cheered on the middle school.

As we all rested,
A friend and I talked.

The infamous group,
I missed yet again.

He asked,
What happened to your wrist?
Are you okay?

With one brain cell working I said,
Gotta Go.

Another conversation was avoided.

Perhaps another low?

Neon Dance

What a day!
What a day.

A race only a day ago.

I woke up at seven and met a friend for breakfast.
Next, I took a short intermission to talk to friends and family.
I procrastinated a bit until I had to prepare for the school dance.

Yes dress.
No dress.
White jeans,
A neon shirt,
And a colorful white plaid-
That was my attire for the dance.
I curled my hair and painted my face.

Did a photo shoot with Dad in front of our garage.
Took a short piano break and then off to the dance.

The room was dark with neon lighting.
Black lights were on and made the room glow.
I took pictures with friends and picked up extra glow.

We started dancing from the start.
I wore a flower crown and a glow stick around my neck.
We were jumping up and down to songs,
Having fun all the while.

We didn't stop until the night was over.

We closed with a classic song.
And I took sweets for the road.

Don't forget this night.
Don't forget the happiness.

PROMPTS FROM OTHERS AND MYSELF

Strawberry

There are rows and rows of strawberries.
Just like the world's possibilities.

Let me fill my box with random strawberries.
Some strawberries may be sour.
And some may be sweet.
When there is a rotten strawberry.
 I simply inspect and deal with it.

My box of strawberries changes daily.
Sometimes all the strawberries are all sour.
And sometimes they're all sweet.

I'll deal with the sour when and whence they come
When I'm dealt the sour strawberries.
I'll keep some and deal with the others.

Foot

They say if you give a person an inch,
They would take a mile.
What if you give them a foot?

Give a depressed person a foot,
And you'll see them in the news.
Give a depressed person an inch,
And they might recover.

If I gave you a foot what would you do?
Would you run to the light or hide in the dark?

You'll get to go home soon.
But you will not be alone.
We're cheering you on from here.
Family and friends are by your side.
Be a light and be a guide..
Others will help you on your way.
Be safe on your way.

Anchor

Once an anchor to a friend.
But now an anchor to lend.

You're rooted and grounded in kindness and empathy.
You stand with a large amount of empathy.
You'll be here for new generations and the old.
You stand with an outstretched hand and spread smiles where you
can.
You're confident and a friend.
You help prevent the end of the road.
You help the broken mend by lending them a helping hand.

News

All wait on bated breath as sadness rolls on the breeze.
The crow watches as the vulture crows.
Not all is as it seems.
Tears stream on the floor and the ground takes it in.

All will be okay.
All will be okay.
All will be okay someday.

Cartoon

Cartoons are exaggerated and easier to relay harshness.
Cartoons are animated and playful.
Cartoons make you smile and laugh.
Thank goodness I'm not a cartoon.

White Walls and a Window

There are four walls and a window.
Shades help the landscape evade my view.
A tall shelf stands lonely in the corner.
The loud door slants down as if attempting to be unthreatening.
The window is to make the room seem open,
As if we weren't in prison.
There's a beep when you leave a door,
And a click when you enter.

I dare you to tell me that this is not a prison.
Tell me that this is okay.

I used to be okay with that,
But now I want out.
I want to leave.
I want to walk the long hallway and breathe in the outside air.

Crescent Moons

I have crescent moons in the palms of my hands.
As the moon in the sky fades and returns,
So do my crescent moons.

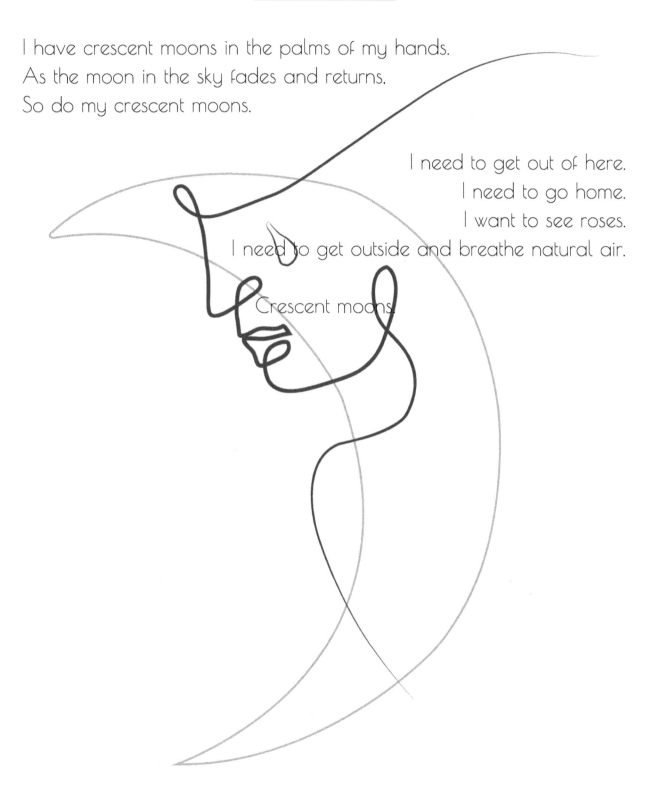

I need to get out of here.
I need to go home.
I want to see roses.
I need to get outside and breathe natural air.

Crescent moons.

Stampede

A stampede can be heard from miles away.
It sounds like thunder that comes from underground.
Is there anything that can compare to a stampede?

No.

Fierce emotions come running silent.
They're formidable.
They're invisible.
They're a spontaneous force.

A barrage of emotions surges in uniform.
Beware.
The silent stampede is at the top of the chain.
Beware.
The stampede is real.

Kite

Let me be a kite.
Let me soar high in the sky.
I'll use my colors to blend in with the sunsets so that you cannot find
me and bring me down.

Let me find my way in the space of the sky.
Let me have my rope.
Let me be free.

Astronomical

Look up!
Look up!
There are thousands of stars!
We are here on earth, but not too far from the stars.

The stress we deal with and create surrounds us.
We need a tension breaker.
We need a knife to slice the air.
That's what we need.
To make a tear.

So,
Look up.
Look up.
The number of stars is astronomical.
Their beauty is safe afar.

The stars do not quarrel.
The stars only speak.
The moon.
The stars.
And the sky can take you away.
They can take you out of your mind.

Become an astronaut.
Become an astronaut.
Even if only for tonight.

Metaphorical

My thoughts are a TRAINWRECK.
PIECES are strewn across the ground.
Raiders come and STEAL my cargo.
Take off and drop the BOMBS.
I don't know who stole my thoughts,
But I guess it doesn't Matter.
This situation is completely METAPHORICAL.
MYSELF.
ME.
And I.
Who stole my THOUGHTS?
Who killed my MIND?
I guess that it was all just ME.
Because in myself,
I am all ALONE.

Wind

The wind carries many stories:
A heap of leaves to leap into.
The sun beating down.
The waves swallowing all the fears.
And songs play loudly.

The wind will carry my story,
Even if I don't sing it aloud.
The wind will guide my story to you so that you may listen too.

Life is not fully planned,
Nor will it ever be.
Listen to the stories in the wind and take what you need.

Beans

How much for three magical beans?

I want the kind of beans that take you to another world.

I want to use the first bean to escape my current reality.

The second bean I'll use in case the escape fails.

The last magic bean will grow on my grave.

I'll use my resting place to help future generations.

They'll use my gift to aid themselves.

I hope my gift helps.

Glass

The glass shatters against the cold floor.
Potential runs through my ideas.

No.

Get those thoughts out of my door.
I can't risk that anymore.

Let me turn my amp up and play loudly.
I climb up frets at different levels.
Let me climb.
Up and down I fall.

Music explodes.
The music is a beautiful and chaotic noise.
Is the music my life?

No.

My life song shatters the glass.
But because I'm climbing the frets the glass vanishes.

My life song is joined by many.
Many frets.
Many strings.

I am NOT ALONE.

<u>Spaced</u>

I am not fully here,
But I am not stuck there.
I am somewhere in between.

Voices are listening keenly.
I am never fully alone.

God is here with his tone.
He is kind.
And gentle.
And loving.
He is also strict.
And fair.
And just.
He is strict and kind when I am deaf.

I am not alone.
There are voices in my head that I can't get rid of.

Bananas

It's time to go bananas.
It's time to have a ball.
It's time to go supernova.

Bananas.
Bananas.
It's time to go bananas.

We're all stuck in this game.
So why not have some fun?
We don't need to stay the same.
We don't need to change.
We don't have to do this or that,
But we all have a chance to.

Bananas.
Bananas.
I think I'll go bananas.

I will not stay the same.
Watch me grow and change.

Beauty

Let the cherry blossoms erupt with beauty.
The pink and white hues are brilliant against the grey skies.
No cherry blossom is alone because they all grow together.
All vines are on one tree.
Yet they all have different stores.
Alone a cherry blossom is beautiful.
But together,
They are stunning.

Gee

Goodness.
Gee.
You can make me so happy.
Your energy is so high.
I think you make the negative say "goodbye."

Your smiles bring smiles.
Your laughs bring laughs.
Strictness ensues chaos.

Gee.
Why do you make me so happy?
You can change others' futures.
You can make people happy.

Aqua

Aqua is such a stunning color.
Bluish-green creates aquamarine.
Aquamarine is the color of the coral.

Coral can be found in the oceans.
Coral houses fish.
Coral is a safe haven for creatures.
Find me an aquamarine coral.
Find it so I can see.

Expendable

Are feelings not expendable?
Are feelings not replaceable?
Are feelings not substitutional?

If I got rid of my feelings,
What would happen?
What would replace feelings?

Numbness.
Numb.
Numbness will replace feelings.
Numbness.
Numb.

Feelings are expendable,
But they're dependable.
They won't attack if you numb them.

Numb.
Numb.
Don't be dumb.

Traitor

The girl in my mind is a traitor.
She's mean.
But I guess I made her.

She's my very own demon.
And you cannot see her.
I think you know that she's here.

How is my girl a traitor?
I can tell you because I made her.
She waits for the panic.
And when it comes a demon.

Let me make another girl.
The girl can help me be calm.
Then she turns around.
And I realize that I now have two demons inside.

Elope

Can I just elope from this place of cold and stone?
Do you want to come with me?
We can run away sublime.
We can cross the threshold of danken dreams and enter reality.
Do you want to run away?
Let's elope from here.

Cherish the Moments

Cherish the moments.
That's what they say to do.

The old and the new,
I can cherish those too.

I should stay in the present and not zone out to space,
But that is much harder than the reality I face.

I hear the thumping that is very much on beat.
It calms me but scares me.
To where should I flee?

I remember the raised voices and the sadness I faced.
I remember dialing and texting in haste.
I remember a lot.
But to the niche.
That's where the memories go.

Cherish the moments.
Cherish the happy moments and the sad ones.
All moments have meaning and value and calm.

Blue

Blue is the universal color of sadness.
But blue is not sadness alone.

Blue is the ocean:
Deep.
Dark.
Full of dangers.

But the ocean has another tone.
The ocean is playful.
The ocean plays with kids and the moon.

The ocean holds colorful things.
Creations to explore.

Blue has so many sides.
Jump into the blue to learn something new.

If I Were my Parents

If I were my parents,
I don't know what I'd do.

If I were my parents,
I'd go up in a spew.

If I were my parents,
I'd ask someone for help.

If I were my parents...
But I'm not my parents.

What Makes Me Mad

I don't know what makes me mad.
I don't know what makes me sad.

All I know is that stress is messy.
Stress is messy.
And that's what gets me.

When fighting between the three occurred,
I used to hide.

Soon the tables turned,
And I was caught in between.
It seemed that the roles were reversed.

Strict rules are put in place.
What is listening at a steady pace?

Friends are judged.
And music too.
School is fine.
But it's a load.

The work,
The studies,
The grades-
They had to be done to code.

Hope was in tow when I confided in friends.

The stress.
The sadness.
The panic I face.
There is much I leave unsaid.
But for now.
What I said.
I leave to be read.

What Happens When I Get Out

What happens when I get out?

Will everything go back to normal?
Will everything be the same?
I don't want anything to change.

Will I have to eat more?
Will I have to stay downstairs?
Will I get my door back?
How about my phone?

I've missed a week of school.
I have not seen my friends.

How will anything be the same?
Did I even change?

I want to go to soccer.
I want to go to drama.
I even want to go to choir.
I want my life back:
The crap and all the drama.

Wish for Wishes to Come True

Can I wish for my wishes to come true?

If I did... Well,what would you do?

What if I wished for a car and a house?
What if I wished for a friend and a spouse?
What if I wished for good grades and no frets?
What if I wished for a good-only net?

What if all of my wishes came true?
Well,what then?
Well, what?
Well, what would you do?

What if my wish car was broken and my house in shambles?
What if my friends are only on the surface?
What if my spouse is angry and violent?
What if my grades are good but stress is ample?
What if my frets are only gone for a while?
What if my net has a huge hole?

What then was the purpose of wishing for wishes?
I do not know why.
Just leave it at that.

I'm Afraid to Ask For

I'm afraid to ask for help.
I'm afraid to ask for a hug.
I'm afraid of conversation.

Why am I afraid?

I'm afraid that they will leave.
I'm afraid that I will be alone.
I'm afraid that I will fall.
I'm afraid that I will drown.

I'm afraid to show my true self.
I'm afraid I don't know who I am.

1st Day of High School

On my first day of high school,
I was confident.
I had my foursome friend group.
There were new kids at school.
We invited a new girl to sit with us at lunch.
Our classes jumped into difficulty.
I remember my first day of high school.
I'm glad that I do.

Checkmate

When you place your pawn on two squares,
It annoys me.
When you point to something and try to move your piece,
I see your trick.
When you let me steal your knight,
I groan with annoyance.

I'm tired of playing your game.
I'm done playing your game.

I reveal my thoughts and feelings between games.
The ticks as you sit there.
I let my words become sharp enough to tear you through.
No one stands with me as the clock rings.
You just sit there silent.
Silent.

Of course I didn't expect anyone else to stand.
Even so,
I leave the board and walk away.

When you hear the others speak up,
You run.

But because I left the board first,
I'm in trouble.

INKTOBER

Crystal

Crystal clear my intentions are.
Crystal clear.
He said.

Crystal clear my love for you.
Shining through and through.

You're a crystal in the rocks.
Hiding just for me.
When he picked me up and smiled.
I smiled within thee.

He used to be a diamond.
Shining ever bright.
But time seemed to bend backward.
And he shone even lighter.
The dullness threw him down.
And he left without a word.

Should I regret him?
Will I ever learn?

Suit

The boy's father is his idol.
He wakes every morning and fixes his suit.
The boy watches the imperfections be smoothed down with a quick movement.
I'll be like him too when I grow old.
Says the boy.

As the boy grows,
He sees loose ties and flashy bow ties.
No need for a suit when more attractive,
Easier things are found.

The grown boy smiles in the mirror as his son watches as he fastens a flashy bow tie.

The suit hangs lonely in the closet...
Maybe to be remembered later,
Or perhaps not.

Vessel

Life is a game.
Or so I was told.
I, A vessel in their game.
And them in mine.
Life is a game that everyone plays.
Whether they like it or not, it continues.
Life is a game in the sense of it going.
In the sense that it is play after play.
I am your vessel.
A small piece.
Yes, it's true.
So, let me make my piece worthwhile.
Let my vessel through.

Knot

Tie a knot around my waist as I dive into the depths.

The ever-seeming darkness is entrancing and alluring.
Not much can survive down here except the creatures of the dark.
I see demons of hate.
Fear.
Loneliness.
Self-deprecation.
Self-harm.
And isolation.

                    Be ready to pull me up when I tug twice.
                    But know that I am not quite ready yet.

Let me sink further.
Further into the depths.

Let me find my insecurities.
My fears.
And my lost hopes.
Let me find the friendships that I yearn for.
But also fear.
Let me find you while I'm at my low.

                    It's time.
                    Pull me up.
                    Pull me up before I drown.

Have you watched the knot?

Will you keep me safe?

Pull me up beside you.

HOLD ME in your arms.

Raven

Perched atop a streetlight,
The raven sings her mournful song.

The raven has seen many a day,
In which the world's happiness has fallen away.

Below,
The raven sees sorrowful scenes:

One of death by loud and discordant machines.
Flashing red and blue lights rush to the noise.

The raven spreads her wings,
Already knowing where to go next.

A fire burning so brightly that it lights up the night.
The flames devour the mansion whole.
Nothing is left once the fire has dwindled.
Everything that once was known is now gone,
EXCEPT for a blood-red rose among the ash.

A light sheet of ash rests on the roses' petals.
The raven swoops down and picks the rose.

The raven carries hundreds of feet above the ground,
And then lets it fly.

Spirit

My spirit is stuck in my body.
But my mind is watching from afar.

The girl begins to tremble.
Trying to suffocate the darkness.
The voices become louder.

My mind backs away.
Further from the scene.

Disassociation.
Flee.
Hide.
Reside in the vast emptiness.

A comforting voice pulls my mind back into my body.
She's here.
She's here.
She may only be here in mind.
But she's here.

I lean into her.
Giving her my spirit and my soul to protect.

She is a reason I get up.
She is a reason I continue on.

What happens when she only becomes a memory?

What happens when she leaves?
What happens if I never take the first step?
What is the first step?

Don't let my spirit die!

I beg you.
Invite me in.

Fan

Endless stars hang in the sky.

Stars are a comfort to the lost,
A salve to the heart,
And hope for the hopeless.

The broken boy loves the stars.
The broken boy wishes to be with them.
The broken boy longs to be one.
The broken boy ties stars to the ceiling fan.

The broken boy listens to the fights outside his door.

The broken boy becomes one with the stars in his room.

The broken boy forgets the world.

The boy is whole.

Watch

Never-ending fields of wheat wave with the wind.
The ever-changing sky foretells adventures,
But the crow cares about one thing only.

The crow only wants a shimmering moment.

The crow soars over the land in search of its prize.

The watch lies alone by the bridge:
Broken glass and mourning hands.

The crow shrieks in pleasure at the glinting treasure.

Mine!

The crow takes the watch for his own.

Two broken things make each other whole within each other.

PRESSURE

all eyes were on me.
no need to count to three.

was i melting into the floor?
had i bolted for the door?

were my secrets spilling out?
wait,
was i talking out loud?

a question was posed.
what response was exposed?

a secret within a safe space.
why was i afraid?

let the pressure break my wall.
let me tell of my shadows now.

my ONCE UPON A TIME...
never spoken a line.

let me tell you my ONCE UPON A TIME when we're both free and
when the pressure is not wholly on me.

Pick

You picked me up and told me to trust you.
You told me that you could be my safe haven.
You promised to hold my life steady.
I believed you.
That was my fault.
You let me plummet.
You fooled me.
You seem as if nothing happened.
Never again.
I said.
Yet I did it again and again.
And now when I need it most.
I battle myself to let another hold me.
Please prove that you're better than them.
Please.

Sour

Sweet or sour,
They say that you can choose.

Happy or sad,
Make your move.

Looking up,
I see rock bottom.

What's below?
I do not know.

Before I begin my climb to the light,
Let me ask:
Why is it so hard to fight?

I've been to where the light is,
But that was long,
Long ago.

Why should I climb?
Why should I go?

I once danced in the light.
I think it was sweet to be in the light,
But now I don't remember.

I dance in the dark now with my demons and my fears.

There's no hope for miles,
or that's how it seems.

Life used to be sweet,
Life used to be hopeful,
Life used to be happy,
But now it is woeful.

Why continue with the "sweet" when there is more sour?

What should I hold on to?
Where should I go?

Stuck

Hope is drawn to the light just as misery is drawn to the dark.

The sun may set on a lit day.
But the next morning is always bright.

When the sun sets on a dark day,
One can only wish it becomes stuck within the in-between.

The light is sweet as a sunrise.
And the dark is frigid as an icy lake.

Trapped beneath the ice.
Living with no oxygen.

Others stride atop the ice.
Living without care.

Few find the holes to the light.
Fewer survive the climb out.
Why am I stuck beneath?

Roof

I was once safe.
As you probably are now.
Safe from the world's cruelty.
Safe from the devil's snare.

I was once shielded from the acidity of loss.
I was once covered by pure ignorance.
I was once like you.
But my roof caved in.

I lost everything that once made me happy.
I watched it all crumble to dust.

Will you be lucky enough to keep the roof over your head.
Or will you be like me?

I hope that your roof stays intact.

T.I.C.K.

Time moves slowly when a fight occurs.
Insecurities flutter through me like butterflies.
Concern etches itself into a buried niche.
Kill time with the business.

T.I.C.K.
T.I.C.K.
T.I.C.K.

Time seems to run forever.
Inside me, a dam builds.
Certainty becomes apprehension.
Kindness is hard to accept.

T.I.C.K.
T.I.C.K.

Trust was broken.
I am an inmate in my own prison.
Constantly darkness tries to bury me six feet under.
Kaleidoscope... that's what my thoughts seem to be.

T.I.C.K.

Turbulent demons harass me.
Instability becomes my friend.
Cornered by my own self.
Knocking at my door is the reaper... of what sort though?

T-I-C-K.

Time has run out.

Helmet

My helmet is made for protection.
My helmet is to keep me safe.

Let me fix your dented helmet,
Or give you mine instead.
Let me save you from acid rain.
Let me give you safety.

You might fear the stormy days.
But I have lived them through.
I have already felt the rain.
I have already been hurt.

Look over all my injuries.
Look over all my sores.

Let me help you when you're in need.
Take my helmet from me.

Compass

A compass will always point true to the north.
A compass will always lead you straight.

Have you ever seen a broken compass?
I bet that you've not ever seen a broken compass.
But I have.

My compass's needle is fickle when guiding.
My compass is shattered.
My compass is broken.
My compass is damaged.

If you are interested in broken things,
Come and visit,
But do not stay for more than a while.

I do not need anything more to misguide my compass.
I do not need false hope.

Come and view my compass.
I have it on display in a glass box.
Almost never does it come out.
I need my compass to remain how it is.

Collide

I'm scared of collision.

When two things collide,
Usually the remnants form something new.
When two things collide it can be great or it can be horrible.
When I collided with darkness it was okay at first.
But then we became one.

I sank.

But then,
I collided with you.

Maybe it was dumb luck,
Or maybe it was a blessing.
Whatever it was,
I am thankful.

We are becoming a weapon,
Forged by darkness to overcome it.

We may fall,
But we will rise.

Our collision will not be overlooked.

We will rise.
We will rise together.

Moon

Hello Moon,
    I see you from my window,
    My barred and solemn window.
    Why do you only show your true colors at night?

Moon, I am tired.
    If I fall asleep under your reign will you keep watch
    over me?

Good morning Moon,
    I'll see you in another few hours.

Loop

It hurts my heart:
Seeing how numerous the sad people are.
Knowing that many people (some of them, my friends) are silently in pain.
Feeling the whiplash from life's curve balls.

It pains me:
To walk every day with motions in hand.
To see the shared point of my downfall.
To second guess the right decision.

Listen:
This loop will end...
I'm not sure exactly when,
But i know,
I hope it will.

Look forward to:
The brighter days.

Look for the:
Small joys.

Fight to:
End the continuous loop that ensnares you.

Ask and seek:
Help from trusted friends.

Sprout

I see a tad of green hidden among the dirt.
I hear you crying aloud for all you're worth.
I see you beginning to come up.

Come up.
Come out.

Show your petals to the world.

I see you taking in all the pain.
I see you growing underneath the sun.
I see the blazing heat and wilting weeds.
But remember that you're not a weed.
You are a flower.
You will stand tall.

Maybe your petals aren't showing yet.
But someday.
They will.

A flower must be a sprout at some point.
Grow into your petals.

Fuzzy

I used to love you so so much,
But now my feelings are fuzzy.
I used to feel warm inside whenever you were around me.
I used to see you in perfect light,
But now your features are blurred.
Nothing in this world is crystal clear...
In fact,
Everything is torn.
Fuzzy are my feelings for you.
You're tearing my heart in two.
I loved you so so much,
But now we keep out of touch.

<u>Open</u>

I CAN'T BREATHE.
SOMETHING SITS HEAVY IN MY CHEST AND INFECTS MY LUNGS.

I CAN'T BREATHE.
THE AIR OUTSIDE IS POLLUTED.
THE SULFUROUS STING BRINGS TEARS TO MY EYES.

I CAN'T BREATHE.
THE SHARP VOICES BRING COMFORT AND A SENSE OF SAFETY.

I CAN'T BREATHE.
I CAN'T BREATHE.
I CAN'T BREATHE.

MEDS BRING CALM SERENITY.
FREEDOM OPENS BEFORE ME AS THE MEDS OVERTAKE MY BRAIN.
BREATHE.

TOMORROW I WON'T BE ABLE TO BREATHE.
BUT FOR NOW.
I CAN BREATHE.

BREATHE.

Leak

I once made a robot out of scrap that I found.
I hooked up the wires and drew on buttons.
I gave him a memory and a pulse and a choice.
But he did not want the life that I "forced".

I felt it briefly.
Only a moment's notice.
But my robot's fuel had a leak in its tank.

I figured out late that it had been on purpose.
He had decided to return to his form from the beginning.

Extinct

There is a creature that is near extinction.
It should be protected with all of your might.
You should make sure no harm befalls this creature.

There is only one made in a variety of different ones.
It is extremely valuable.

We must protect this creature.
We must be in love with this creature.

Have you guessed what this creature is?
IT IS YOU.
There is only one of you.
Protect and love yourself and others around you.

Splat

Humpty Dumpty went splat on the ground.
Humpty Dumpty fell off of his wall.
Humpty Dumpty was broken and shattered.
I am like Humpty Dumpty once after.

Humpty Dumpty was broken but then repaired.
Humpty Dumpty had help and some care.
I am like Humpty Dumpty, with help.
I am not alone to face the breaking of self.

Connect

My life is a giant puzzle.
All the pieces connect.
I do not know all the pieces at once,
But they all fit in perfectly.

Some of the pieces are ragged and torn.
Some of the pieces look perfect.
But no matter what the pieces look like they all fit into my life.

My puzzle is mine.
Yes, it isn't perfect.
But my puzzle is my puzzle alone.
And for that,
I am wholly grateful.

Spark

There is a spark in your eyes as you tell me your story.
Your eyes darken as you speak about your hurt.
Sorrow
And pain.

Once you finish telling your story,
Your eyes gleam with relief.
You have moved my heart to tears.

A burden that was once held by you alone is now shared.
Others gladly help you hold the weight of life.

I'm so proud of you.
I'm so proud that you've decided to ask for help.

Crispy

No chicken wants to end up in a crispy chicken tender box.
But some do.

They can't control what happens to them.
But we can partially control what happens to us.

There is always a choice for us to make.
There is always a crossroads where we must make a choice.

Let's be grateful that we're not chickens.
We're people with choices and free will.

HARD TRUTH

Mask

Yeah.
I wear a mask sometimes...
Let's be honest.
We all wear a mask at some point.

Lies and Truth

Lies:

The day just repeats over and over.

These white washed walls are all the same.

What is the point?

I make no difference.

I put myself out there and no one notices.

My voice is not heard.

It's out of pity.

I'm alone.

No one will understand.

They'll leave if they know.

Nothing will ever get better.

Truth:

Every day can be special...

You just have to see it.

The whole story is not yet revealed.

People don't know what your want,

So just ask them.

Don't whisper.

Shout it out.

It's out of love.

They might understand.

Good friends will stay and listen.

It will get better (one step at a time).

It will overwhelm you if you ignore it.

People can help you...

All you need to do is ask.

Just One

Just One...
Just one moment.
Just one act.
Just one word.
Just one hug.
Just one friend.
Just one smile.
Just one laugh.
Can change someone's mind.

Hold On To Friends

Friends...
When life gets tough they stay with you.
When you become confused they help you through.
When you are hurting they hold your hand.
When you fall they reach out to help you up.
When you cry they are beside your with empathy.
When you need a smile they help you find one.
When you want to give up they won't let you.
When you ask they will answer honestly.
Should be held onto.
Are special.

Facades

Facades:
The wall that you've held up for so long needs to go.
Hold you back from amazing opportunities.
Hide the truth from those who care.
Limit the amount someone can learn about you.
Are detrimental to your mental health.
Kill your self-esteem.
Have repercussions.
Don't stop those who care about you.
Need to be lowered.

<u>Time</u>

It's time...
To speak up for someone.
To be the voice that disagrees with the world.
To call out to the lost.
To go against the familiar current of life.
To ask for guidance.
To reach out in kindness to the world's outcasts.
To lead the lost to the Father.
To live for God.

Grey Skies

Gray skies...
When the sky is gray the sun is hiding.
When the sky is gray the warmth is gone.
When the sky is gray the clouds are dark.
When the sky is gray the shade is plentiful.
When the sky is gray the clouds bring rain.
When the sky is gray you can always find shining rays of light.
Are beautiful.

Curve Ball

Curve Balls:
Come out of the blue.
Threaten all your plans.
Throw you for a loop.
Can ruin your week.
Make you do a double take.
Can make your heart break.
Can help you grow.
Make your head spin.
Are obstacles to be overcome/
Can be hit.

105 Minutes

105 minutes to sleep,
The rest of the time to think.
Why is time so slow?
I feel like I use it up like so:
I draw and I paint,
I read the Word,
I listen to music,
But still I become bored.
105 minutes until a new day.

Thunder-Struck

Thunder-

Drowns out the rest.
Is accompanied by light.
Scares the young.
Destruction ensues.
Is an orchestra.
Is a beautiful sound.
Is a wonder.
-Struck

The Story

There are two sides to every story.
Though one side may be more blurry.

One may think that they are right,
But the other disagree with the same exact might.
One will end up hurt and offended,
While the other knows not of the hurt they extended.

There are no right ways to end the hurt...
Except to speak and apologize first.

One cannot when they hurt one another.
So one must speak up-nicely-
To their sister or brother.

<u>Things To Remember</u>

People don't know how you want them to respond.
So tell them what you truly want.

You can be tired.
But you can't give up.

Secrets can be detrimental to your health.

Hold on to your real friends.

Facades need to be lowered.

Lies build until they hurt.

The unexpected can be turned around.

It's okay to ask for help.

<u>Don't Give Up</u>

There are days when you can't find the good.
Find a friend who will help you through.
The good is there.
You just have to look.

When there are gray clouds, make them white.
Find joy in the small.
Don't give up on life.

Is This You

I've built my wall too high.
The things that I've fought off just return.
My guard has been up for too long.
When will it all end?
I'm tired of fighting.
I'm tired of lying.
I'm tired of putting up an act.
I am exhausted.
Home can't come soon enough.

There is hope.
It will get better in time.
People can help you.
Just let down your guard and open your heart.

Content

I can be happy here
No pressures
No worries
Darkness at bay
Here I can just be

Acknowledgements:

I want to thank Amanda R for being my mentor. Amanda was the girl's youth director for many years. My first sleepaway camp was a youth retreat (and it was unknown territory). Amanda was always there when I felt homesick and a person to talk to. Amanda was also a person who was an integral group of people who helped me overcome depression and find my faith. Amanda, thank you for being my mentor and friend.

I want to thank Rachel M for being a great friend and mentor during my season of depression. Rachel was the person that I entrusted an unexpected dark encounter with. The encounter was with someone that I thought that I could trust and depend on, but I was extremely wrong. Rachel was my best friend when my support system crumbled along with the relationship with the person who ended up being untrustworthy. Rachel, thank you so much for guiding me in my faith, being my mentor, and someone that I can trust with anything.

Meiyin is quirky, thoughtful and relationship focused. She puts effort and focus into trying to know others and showing them that they are meaningful to her. She does this in only a Meiyin, unique way. She has one of a kind ideas to make her friends and family feel valued and loved. Meiyin is ambiguous, artistic, adventurous, creative and a deep thinker. Most importantly, she has a spiritual maturity and desire to love and grow in the Lord.
~Mike V

Mike is an amazing man who loves God. He was my youth pastor for quite a few years. Mike never failed to make me smile in any, and every, situation. When Mike became the youth pastor he brought his charismatic personality and boundless energy. With 'Big Mike' around there is no one alone or excluded from a group. Mike, thank you for bringing the youth group closer and closer to God and community.

Amber V, Mike V's wife also deserves a thanks. I look up to Amber's gentleness and listening skills. She listens without judgement, is gentle (but firm) with the truth, and responds in a respective way that makes you know that she wants what is best for you. Amber, thank you for being a good listener and an amazing friend.

Remember that party a while ago when I dared you $5 to jump into the pool fully clothed? Then you actually did it and dared me to jump in too. I'm still thankful for the pink flower cookie you shared with me in 2nd grade at recess.
~Zoe R

I want to thank Zoe R for being my close friend. She never fails to push herself when we hang out. She loves me so much that she endures riding her bike with me to different places. Zoe is a great person who puts up with my shenannigins. I am so glad that her family puts up with me randomly walking

INTO THEIR HOUSE. I LOVE HANGING OUT WITH ZOE AND TALKING ABOUT LIFE AND FAITH. THANK YOU ZOE FOR BEING MY BESTEST CLOSEST FRIEND.

I WANT TO THANK 'ME^2': MAKENNA G, EMILY H, AND EMMA O. ME^2 HAS BEEN A FRIEND GROUP SINCE SEVENTH GRADE. EVEN THOUGH WE EVENTUALLY ENDED UP GOING TO DIFFERENT HIGH SCHOOLS WE HAVE KEPT OUR FRIENDSHIP. ALTHOUGH SEVERAL WEEKS AND MONTHS PASSED BETWEEN OUR LAST GET TOGETHER, WHEN WE SAW EACH OTHER WE ACTED AS IF WE WERE NEVER DISTANCED. WE HAVE ALWAYS HAD SOMETHING TO SHARE WITH EACH OTHER WHEN WE HUNG OUT. MY FRIENDSHIP WITH EACH PERSON IN THE GROUP IS SOMETHING THAT I WOULD NOT TRADE A MILLION DOLLARS FOR. THANK YOU GUYS FOR BEING SOME OF THE BEST FRIENDS THAT I HAVE EVER HAD!

MEIYIN IS A CREATIVE AND FEARLESS SPIRIT. SEEKING THE CONNECTION IN LIFE, SHE GIVES HER ALL TO EVERYTHING SHE DOES! GENUINE, CARING, AND RELATIONAL - THAT IS MEIYIN.
~ASHLEY H

MEIYIN IS FUNNY, FRIENDLY AND COMPASSIONATE. IN ONE MOMENT SHE CAN TAKE YOU FROM LAUGHTER TO MINDFUL TO COMPASSION.
~JASON T

I WANT TO THANK ASHLEY H, JAKE F, DAVID E, MEGAN C, MRS. D, JASON T, AND ROB T. ALL OF THESE PEOPLE WERE A HOME AWAY FROM HOME. THEY WERE MY SPIRITUAL SUPPORTS WHEN I WAS AWAY FROM HOME. THEY WELCOMED ME into their church family and their hearts. They made me laugh and cry and feel at home. Besides these special people I want to specifically thank everyone from New Journey Church (Wabash, In). New Journey is a welcoming church that taught me many things and made me a part of their family. New Journey Church and its people are a home that I will never forget. I will forever cherish the memories and relationships that I made there. Thank you everyone from New Journey and Ashley H, Jake F, David E, Megan C, Jason T, and Rob T. Thank you Ashley for loving me, listening to me, and guiding me. Thank you Jake for being the funny person that you are... treating me like I was always a part of your church family (but I suggest that you eat your fruit). Thank you David for being an incredible chef, a caring person, and someone that takes care of everyone in such a way that makes them feel special. Thank you Megan for letting me love Makenna. Megan, you are truly a kind person who made me feel at home at camp... thank you. Thank you Mrs. D for being a really cool person to talk to, having a cool husband that works sound, and for leading people in worship. Thank you Jason for being a funny person to be around. You're not old, but you do have a sense of humor that not every person has. Rob, you're a really good pastor who has taught me a lot. I must say that the small golfing green in your office is broken. It seems to not accept the golf ball every time for me, but every time for you. I must say that it seems to be bias to whos golf ball it accepts. Thank you all for being people that have impacted my life in such a positive way.

"Are you sure about this? It's like less than 50 degrees." "Oh yeah it's worth it." And that's when Meiyin threw the ball into the lake. My dogs, ran after it, excited and determined, until that is a wave hit them and pushed them back to shore. Welp. I guess there goes a good ball. Splash! Just kidding Meiyin, runs into the freaking cold water to retrieve the ball herself. And I think this story says a lot about Meiyin as she had to trek out into the water. Meiyin is fearless, and also humble. She recognized her error and decided to fix it, as I (as well as the dogs and anyone else at the park) watched her freeze herself to retrieve a 25 cent ball. Meiyin's determination has always been a characteristic of her that has been seen. I think about the time the TV wasn't working and everyone bored in the house couldn't

FIND SOMETHING TO DO. MEIYIN TOOK THE DOGS INTO HER ROOM, WITH HER TYPICAL MISCHIEVOUS SMILE, AND CAME BACK 20 MINUTES LATER WITH THE DOGS FULLY CLOTHED IN HER CLOTHES (SOCKS INCLUDED). MEIYIN IS CREATIVE AND ABLE TO TURN ANY BAD SITUATION FUN. MOST IMPORTANTLY MEIYIN IS CARING AND LOVING. TIME AND TIME AGAIN I SAW HERSELF CONSOLE OTHERS, ENCOURAGE THEM, AND PUSH HERSELF TO BE THE BEST PERSON SHE CAN BE. SHE IS A LEADER AND LOVES TO SERVE OTHERS. MEIYIN IS RESILIENT AND HAS OVERCOME MORE THAN MOST. SHE IS GOOFY, AND SASSY MOST OF THE TIME. SHE CAN BE MOODY LIKE MOST PEOPLE, BUT IS GOOD AT APOLOGIZING WHEN SHE KNOWS SHE IS IN THE WRONG. I KNOW THIS COLLECTION WAS WRITTEN FROM HER HEART, AND BECAUSE OF THAT IT WILL BE SOMETHING YOU CAN'T MISS.

~HALEAH H

I WANT TO THANK HALEAH BECAUSE SHE WAS A GREAT SUPPORT TO ME IN A HARD TIME. SHE GAVE THE HARD TRUTH AND REMINDED ME WHO I AM WHEN I FORGOT. HALEAH TAUGHT ME ABOUT GRACE AND UNDERSTANDING THROUGH DEMONSTRATION. I AM SO GLAD THAT I HAD THE OPPORTUNITY TO BECOME FRIENDS WITH HALEAH BECAUSE SHE IS TRULY A GREAT FRIEND AND AN AMAZING INFLUENCE. HALEAH, THANK YOU FOR BEING AN AUTHENTIC AND HONEST FRIEND.

I WANT TO THANK HANNAH B, SKYLAR C, AND SOPHIA P FOR BEING SOME OF THE BEST FRIENDS THAT I HAVE EVER HAD. THEY WERE A STEADY SUPPORT WHEN I WAS AT A LOW, A FAITHFUL FRIEND WHEN TIMES WERE GOOD, AND FUN FRIENDS ALL THE WHILE. THANK YOU ALL FOR BEING THE AMAZING FRIENDS THAT YOU ARE.

WE ARE WRITING TO EXPRESS OUR DEEPEST APPRECIATION FOR YOUR POETRY BOOK, "POEMS ON EVERY PAGE." YOUR WORDS HAVE TOUCHED OUR HEARTS AND STIRRED OUR EMOTIONS IN WAYS WE CANNOT ADEQUATELY EXPRESS. YOUR

DEDICATION TO YOUR FAMILY AT THE BEGINNING OF THE BOOK RESONATED WITH US. THE GRATITUDE YOU EXPRESSED FOR THEIR SUPPORT AND GUIDANCE REMINDED US OF THE IMPORTANCE OF LOVED ONES IN OUR LIVES. IT IS A BEAUTIFUL TESTAMENT TO THE POWER OF FAMILY AND THE ROLE THEY PLAY IN SHAPING OUR PATHS. ~Publishing Team

Thank you for reading *POEMS ON EVERY PAGE*. It has truly been an adventure writing each and every poem. I hope that in some way I was able to connect with you.

words2relate@gmail.com.

Printed in the USA
CPSIA information can be obtained
at www.ICGtesting.com
LVHW081358220124
769411LV00142B/1701

9 781916 852068